effective literacy practices in **FSL**

making connections

Anderson • Carr • Lewis • Salvatori • Turnbull

foreword by Jim Cummins

PEARSON

Professional
Learning

effective literacy practices in FSL: making connections
Professional Development Book

Publisher: Susan Howell
Product Manager: Diane Masschaele
Managing Editor: Anita Reynolds MacArthur
Project/Developmental Editor: Elaine Gareau
Coordinating Editor: Marie Kocher
Copy Editor: Rosina Daillie
Art Director: Zena Denchik
Designer: David Cheung
Production Coordinator: Shonelle Ramserran
Vice-President Publishing and Marketing: Mark Cobham

ISBN 13: 978-0-321-46945-8
ISBN 10: 0-321-46945-3

Printed in Canada

5 WC 12 11 10

Contents

About the Authors. 4

Acknowledgements 6

Components at a Glance 7

Foreword 8

Ways to Use this FSL Resource 12

Setting the Context: Literacy in FSL 18

Big Ideas

1. Engaging and Motivating Students:
   Making it Real. 26
2. Integrating Oral Language:
   Communicating for Success 36
3. Developing Language Awareness:
   Discovering Patterns. 46
4. Assessing and Differentiating:
   Reaching All Learners 54
5. Activating Strategies:
   Making Connections 62

Comprehension Strategies 72

1. Ask Questions: *Je pose des questions* 74
2. Make Predictions: *Je fais des prédictions* 78
3. Monitor and Repair Comprehension: *Je vérifie
   ma compréhension* 84
4. Make Connections: *Je fais des liens* 90
5. Visualize: *Je vois une image dans ma tête* 94
6. Summarize: *J'identifie l'idée principale* 98
7. Synthesize: *Je fais la synthèse* 104
8. Analyze and Evaluate: *Je réfléchis* 108

Appendices

A. Tactics and Organizers to Support the Big Ideas. 112
B. Glossary 143
C. References and Further Reading 150
D. Index. 155

About the Authors

Bev Anderson, M.Ed.

- National FSL Educational Consultant;
- Former Educational Consultant, Intensive French, Saskatchewan Learning;
- Former Provincial FSL Consultant, Saskatchewan Learning;
- Sessional Lecturer, Faculty of Education, University of Regina;
- Former FSL (Grades 4–12) and ESL Teacher;
- Facilitator of FSL teacher training courses, including Intensive French;
- Co-author of *Intensive French: Interprovincial Teachers' Guide* (2005);
- Author of *Core French: A Curriculum Guide for the Secondary Level* (1997), Saskatchewan Learning;
- Co-author of FSL classroom resources including *En direct*;
- Former President of the Canadian Association of Second Language Teachers (CASLT).

Wendy Carr, Ed.D.

- Coordinator of the French Teacher Education Program, University of British Columbia;
- Elementary FSL Teacher, Coquitlam School District, British Columbia;
- Intensive French Helping Teacher, Surrey School District;
- President, British Columbia Association of Teachers of Modern Languages;
- National Council Helper, Canadian Association of Second Language Teachers (CASLT);
- Co-author and Author of elementary FSL classroom resources including *Visages 1*; *Visages: Assessment Package—National Edition*;
- Creator of Canadian second language teachers' Web site.

Cynthia Lewis, Ph.D.

- National Educational Consultant;
- Former Assistant Superintendent, Director of Instruction, and Principal, Surrey School District #36, British Columbia;
- Researcher of literacy initiatives in 12 schools, British Columbia School Improvement Grant Program;
- Former Elementary and Secondary FSL Teacher;
- Teacher-educator in pre-service, in-service, and postgraduate education, Simon Fraser University;
- Co-author of curriculum guides and FSL classroom resources including *Voyages 1* and *Voyages 2*;
- Research interests include second language teaching and learning theory and practice, and communities of collaborative inquiry.

Michael Salvatori, Ph.D.

- Coordinator of Membership Services at the Ontario College of Teachers;
- Teacher at the Canadian College in Italy and in France with Global Journeys' Summer Enrichment Program affiliated with Appleby College;
- Former FSL Teacher, Consultant, and Administrator with the London Catholic District School Board: Elementary and Secondary FSL Teacher; Curriculum Coordinator of Modern Languages and the Arts; Elementary Principal;
- Co-author of numerous FSL classroom resources including *Sans frontières*; *À la page 1 et 2*; *On y va! 1 et 2*; *Ça marche! 2*; *Nouvelles frontières*; and *Quoi de neuf?*

Miles Turnbull, Ph.D.

- Associate Professor, Faculty of Education, University of Prince Edward Island: FSL pre-service program, French Immersion program, and leadership and learning graduate program;
- President of the Canadian Association of Second Language Teachers (CASLT);
- Former Assistant Professor, Modern Language Centre, Ontario Institute for Studies in Education (OISE), University of Toronto;
- Author and Co-editor of numerous publications, including academic journals, books, articles, reviews, and technical reports;
- Research interests include FSL, code switching, teacher development, teacher belief systems, project-based and experiential learning, and educational technology;
- Research funded by the Social Sciences and Humanities Research Council of Canada, Canadian Heritage, The Education and Quality Assurance Office of Ontario, and the Canadian Association of Second Language Teachers (CASLT).

Acknowledgements

Advisory and Development Team

Jim Cummins, Ph. D.

Contributing Author, Foreword

- Internationally renowned leader in second-language learning and literacy development research;

- Canada Research Chair, Department of Curriculum, Teaching and Learning of the Ontario Institute for Studies in Education (OISE), University of Toronto;

- Author of numerous books, chapters, professional articles, forewords, reviews, academic papers, and technical reports. His most recent book is *Literacy, Technology, and Diversity: Teaching for Success in Changing Times* (with Kristin Brown and Dennis Sayers);

- Research focus includes literacy development in multilingual school contexts, and the potential roles of technology in promoting language and literacy development.

Callie Mady, Ph. D.

Senior Advisor

- Instructor of FSL methodology, Ontario Institute for Studies in Education (OISE), University of Toronto;

- Elementary FSL Teacher; Secondary Teacher of FSL, Spanish, ESL, and Cooperative Education; Secondary School Department Head of French, International Languages, and ESL; International Languages Resource Teacher;

- Co-author of the Ontario Ministry's Grades 9 and 10 Course Profiles and the Grades 9 and 10 Independent French courses;

- Author of numerous professional articles and Co-author/Advisor of FSL classroom resources, including *Quoi de neuf?*

Many educators participated in the development of this professional development resource. Pearson would like to thank the following professionals, who have contributed their time and expertise.

Katy Arnett, Ph.D.
St. Mary's College of Maryland
St. Mary's City, Maryland, U.S.A.

Luba Banuke
Simon Fraser University
Burnaby, British Columbia

Judy Bilenki
St. James-Assiniboia S.D.
Winnipeg, Manitoba

Janet Brine
École Laronde Elementary
S.D. #36, Surrey
Surrey, British Columbia

John Erskine
Winnipeg S.D.
Winnipeg, Manitoba

Jane Jonah
District #2
Moncton, New Brunswick

Sylvianne Kohl
Halton C.D.S.B.
Burlington, Ontario

Teresa Love
French International languages,
Instructional Services
Calgary R.C.S.S.D. #1
Calgary, Alberta

Susan MacDonald
Strait Regional S.B.
Port Hastings, Nova Scotia

Catherine Murray
Thames Valley D.S.B.
London, Ontario

Cathie Peters
S.D. #73, Kamloops/Thompson
Kamloops, British Columbia

Gail Phillips
Faculty of Education
Brock University
Hamilton, Ontario

Richard M. Rice
S.D. #6, NB
Rothesay, New Brunswick

Stephanie Rincker
Regina Public S.D. #4
Regina, Saskatchewan

Ronald Sirois
St. Paul's R.C.S.S.D. #20
Saskatoon, Saskatchewan

Maureen Smith
Faculty of Education
University of Western Ontario
London, Ontario

Stacey Sveistrup
Dr. R.E. McKechnie Elementary
School
Vancouver S.B., District #39
Vancouver, British Columbia

Brian Svenningsen
Toronto D.S.B.
Toronto, Ontario

Josie Varone
St. Joseph Catholic School
York C.D.S.B.
Aurora, Ontario

Components at a Glance

Effective literacy practices in FSL: making connections provides several components to support FSL teachers in their professional learning.

Component	Use this component if you are looking for...
Professional Development Book 	• suggestions for ways to use this resource. • an introduction defining literacy and its application to FSL. • five (5) connected and interrelated Big Idea modules: *Engaging and Motivating Students, Integrating Oral Language, Developing Language Awareness, Assessing and Differentiating,* and *Activating Strategies.* • *Professional Learning Surveys* to facilitate personal reflection on effective literacy teaching practices. • support for explicit teaching of *Comprehension Strategies* for listening, viewing, and reading. • graphic organizers, support for tactics, scaffolding, language development, differentiation, and assessment. • glossary (terms provided in French and English). • professional references and further reading.

Professional Development e-Book 	• an electronic version of the PD Book.
	• video-based professional development:
	  – authentic video of Canadian FSL classroom teachers as they demonstrate literacy instruction within the gradual release of responsibility framework;
	  – video clips of leading Canadian FSL educators as they provide their insights and perspectives on current research, literacy theory, and best practices in the FSL classroom;
	  – video clips of teachers, administrators, and students reflecting on their teaching and learning;
	  – pop-ups of practical classroom tips and activities.
	• modifiable black-line masters for graphic organizers.

Facilitator's Guide 	• facilitator notes, activities, and black-line masters. • materials for use with small group, school-based, or district-wide professional learning communities. • CD-ROM providing presentation slides and modifiable black-line masters.

Foreword

Until very recently, it was rare to see literacy issues being addressed in policies or professional resources dealing with Core French. This professional learning resource breaks new ground in highlighting how FSL teachers can help students harness the conceptual knowledge and literacy strategies they already possess in first or additional languages for purposes of expanding their knowledge of French. By the same token, the reading, writing, and aural skills that students develop in the French class can enhance their literacy development across the curriculum. A considerable amount of research suggests that learning a second language can increase students' overall linguistic awareness and literacy knowledge in their first language.

The core insight underlying this FSL professional resource is that *learning is all about making connections*—between new information and prior experience, between learning strategies employed in one area of the curriculum and those that can be applied in learning other curricular content, and between knowledge and vocabulary encoded in one language and what is being taught in another.

Why has literacy development not been a strong focus of Core French up to this point? A variety of factors have contributed to the lack of connection between Core French teaching and literacy. In many elementary school contexts, FSL is taught by a specialist teacher while literacy is taught by the classroom teacher in the context of Language Arts. Also, FSL teachers have frequently not been included in discussions of literacy policies and practices among school staff because of the perception that these curricular areas have very little to do with each other. Similarly, at the secondary level, literacy remains firmly entrenched as a core focus of the English curriculum (or, in Quebec, the French curriculum), isolated from the teaching of additional languages. The sporadic calls from policy-makers and educators over the past 30 years to teach language and literacy across the curriculum made some inroads into the teaching of content areas, such as Social Studies, Science, and Mathematics, but were seldom heard or heeded within the relatively isolated FSL classroom.

In addition, FSL curricula and instructional approaches drew their inspiration from communicative language teaching that was frequently interpreted as mandating maximum use of the target language with a primary focus on speaking and listening rather than reading and writing. Reading and writing were considered more difficult and less communicative than speaking and listening and thus, there has tended to be little emphasis on extensive reading or on writing for authentic purposes within the FSL classroom.

The goal of maximizing target language use discouraged any cross-lingual reference to English, with the result that vocabulary knowledge, learning strategies, and concepts that students possessed in their first language (L1) were seldom invoked as cognitive tools for learning the L2. Thus, students' attention was rarely drawn to the extensive array of cognate relationships between French and English which derive from their common origins in Latin and Greek. This represents a missed opportunity not only to promote French language development but also to enhance students' knowledge of *English* vocabulary. Because the Latin- and Greek-based lexicon in English consists of relatively low-frequency words, the learning of cognate connections in French can expand students' English vocabulary.

These common assumptions about the nature of communicative language teaching (CLT) are not necessarily shared by those who championed this approach. Sandra Savignon (2000), for example, points out that the "principles of CLT apply equally to reading and writing activities that involve readers and writers engaged in the interpretation, expression, and negotiation of meaning." Nina Spada's overview of the current status of CLT noted that "[s]ensible arguments can be (and have been) made for the principled use of L1 in L2 classrooms and there is theoretical, empirical, and pedagogical support for it" (2007). Thus, while researchers agree that every effort should be made to use the target language for the bulk of instruction within the classroom, there is also some consensus that space should exist for what Miles Turnbull (2001) calls "judicious" use of students' L1 for certain instructional purposes, such as making connections with vocabulary and language structures that students already know in their first language.

The rationale for using written text as a significant input medium for teaching French is straightforward. Most students in the elementary grades already have literacy skills developed in English and so reading itself does not have to be taught. In addition, when compared to the rapid (and disappearing) flow of oral language in the classroom, on the radio or television, or in movies, written language remains available for study, review, and analysis over time, thereby enabling students to use a variety of resources and strategies to figure out the meaning, e.g., dictionaries, inferencing meaning from context, etc. Technological advances in recent years have also made it easier to review and analyze audio texts, e.g., on CD, DVD, or Web pages using similar strategies.

We should also take account of the voluminous research literature showing that extensive reading, in both L1 and L2 contexts, is highly effective in expanding students' vocabulary knowledge and reading comprehension in the target language (see Krashen, 2004, for a review). In fact, research on student achievement that has been carried out in almost 30 countries by the Organization for Economic Cooperation and Development (OECD) shows that *reading engagement* emerged as the strongest predictor of reading comprehension among 15-year olds.

Reading engagement incorporates three distinct components:

- amount and range of reading and writing;
- use of effective strategies for deep understanding of text;
- positive affect and identity investment in reading and writing.

In order for students to learn from target language text, both written and aural, they need to develop and use a range of strategies designed to make the input comprehensible. They also need encouragement and motivation to make the effort to grapple with the meaning. The good news is that all of the elements that contribute to reading engagement are inter-related and feed off each other. Successful reading strategies enable students to read more and, as they read and understand more of the target language, their success generates feelings of accomplishment and fuels the motivation to continue reading and interacting in the target language.

The five Big Ideas that form the foundation of *effective literacy practices in FSL: making connections* explain how to engage and motivate students and how to integrate oral and written language so that one modality reinforces the other. Concrete strategies are also provided on how to assess *for* learning and to differentiate instruction to address the needs of all learners. The Comprehension Strategies section that follows focuses on enabling students to use their cognitive resources for maximum effect through efficient use of learning strategies and to build up their awareness of how the target language works. In other words, *effective literacy practices in FSL: making connections* gives students the tools to become increasingly autonomous learners, gradually gaining the confidence required to engage with oral, written, and visual texts of all kinds in French beyond the immediate curriculum, e.g., on French-language Web sites for project work. Building on this foundation, students are then supported in transforming the input into actual oral and written use of French for authentic purposes.

What I personally find most exciting about *effective literacy practices in FSL: making connections* is that it applies to the teaching of French everything we know about how people learn, thereby opening up new opportunities for students to engage actively with the language and simultaneously expand their literacy and cognitive abilities.

Jim Cummins
Toronto, May 2007

References for the Foreword

Krashen, S. D. *The Power of Reading: Insights from the Research. 2nd edition.* Portsmouth, NH: Heinemann, 2004b.

Organization for Economic Cooperation and Development. *Messages from PISA 2000.* Paris: Organization for Economic Cooperation and Development, 2004b.

Savignon, S. J. "Communicative Language Teaching." In M. Byram (Ed.) *Routledge Encyclopedia of Language Teaching and Learning.* London: Routledge, (2000): 124–129.

Spada, N. Communicative Language Teaching: Current Status and Future Prospects. In J. Cummins and C. Davison (Eds.), *International Handbook of English Language Teaching.* New York: Springer Science + Business Media LLC, (2007): 271–288.

Turnbull, M. There is a role for the L1 in second and foreign language teaching, but... *The Canadian Modern Language Review,* 57 (2001): 531–540.

Ways to Use this FSL Resource

The 2006 research report on teaching French as a Second Language (FSL) indicates that French teachers need information and resources to improve their teaching and cope with the challenges faced in their classrooms (Lapkin, MacFarlane, and Vandergrift, 2006). As FSL teachers, we know that improving our teaching is an ongoing process and we are constantly searching for appropriate materials to support and assist us.

As well, Frank Serafini (2006), a leading researcher and educator in literacy development, indicates that the quality of the classroom teacher, not the resources available to the teacher, is the most important variable in determining effectiveness. He suggests that no significant change in teaching occurs until the teacher also modifies his or her theoretical understandings. This calls for teachers to become reflective practitioners, that is, to reflect on their practice and have many opportunities to develop their theory through first-hand experience.

The purpose of *effective literacy practices in FSL: making connections* is to provide FSL teachers with materials and new information to motivate and engage students and to help them learn French. It will also provide them with opportunities to reflect on their practice and engage themselves in continuous professional learning with support.

The various components of this resource are intended to support the flexible ways in which teachers may choose to use them. The content of the Print Book and e-Book is organized in a linear fashion, and may be used in this way or on a "need to know" basis. The Facilitator's Guide contains study group activities and discussion starters.

FSL teachers may choose to use this FSL resource in a variety of settings:

- as a resource for self-directed learning;
- as part of a professional learning community;
- as a tool for action research in either self-directed learning or professional learning communities;
- as a resource in a pre-service or in-service setting.

Self-directed Learning

Individual FSL teachers may benefit from using this resource in a self-directed manner. They may find it useful to consult Big Ideas 1–5 and the Comprehension Strategies in this book, use the lesson sequences, and view the classroom video clips in the e-Book when planning their lessons. Using the resource in an independent manner allows teachers to dip into any one of the components at their own pace and in their own time.

Self-directed learning does not exclude the possibility of reflective practice. Reflection and personalization are encouraged through the Professional Learning Surveys which are found at the end of this section, as well as at the end of Setting the Context and Big Ideas 1–5. Teachers may also videotape a lesson and self-assess the results or ask a colleague or administrator to observe a particular aspect of their teaching. In this way, individual teachers may use this resource to improve their practice.

> "Continuous learning is often complex and delicate, given the demands that large numbers of students place on the FSL teacher's time. It is worthwhile for teachers, none-the-less, to engage in reflective practice, as longitudinal studies of groups of FSL teachers engaged in curriculum implementation have shown that the value of learning communities lies in the sense making of new practices that participants collaboratively share.
>
> *(Lewis, 1995; Turnbull, 1998; Carr, 2007)*

Professional Learning Communities

FSL teachers may also use this resource as part of a learning community. Research indicates that student achievement is improved in the long term when teachers work together in collaboration to discuss literature and research, plan action, and reflect upon practice in such a way as to continuously refine instruction (Stoll, Fink, and Earl, 2003). Unfortunately, FSL teachers often find themselves teaching in isolation because they are the only FSL teacher, or one of a few FSL teachers, in a particular school. School districts or teacher associations may wish to organize learning community settings for FSL teachers to provide them with an opportunity to discuss effective practices, learn about emerging ideas, and share concerns and successes along the way. This resource provides materials to support teacher leaders in coaching and mentoring roles.

At the same time, FSL teachers may wish to become an integral part of the school-based literacy learning community, and provide a second-language learning perspective. This resource gives them a common literacy vocabulary with which to discuss school literacy with colleagues in such a setting.

Action Research

When teachers introduce new teaching practices into their classrooms, assess those experiences, and draw conclusions which inform their practice, they are engaged in action research. Also called "teacher inquiry" and "reflective practice," action research encourages teachers to learn from their experiences, and apply what they learn to continuously refine their instruction to better meet the needs of their students.

The diagram on the next page (Figure 1) is adapted from the Gordon Wells model (Wells, 1994) as it pertains to professional growth and improves student learning. Teachers may choose to use this model to explore the five modules (Big Ideas 1–5) and the Comprehension Strategies that are presented in this resource. They may individually or collaboratively discuss current practice, view and analyse the classroom video clips in the e-Book which model the practices under discussion, and then try out the lesson sequences.

> " And it is in making the connections between practice and theory, as this relationship is constructed and made explicit through the cycle of research, that the practitioner adopts the stance of reflectiveness, which is the hallmark of the teacher researcher. "
>
> *(Atwell, 1992; Wells, 1994)*

Figure 1

Action Research

• Make systematic observations
  of the situation to determine
  what is actually happening.

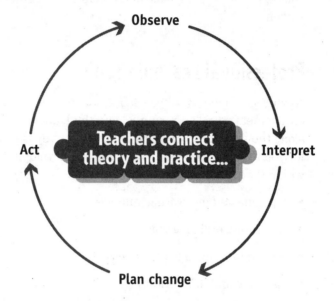

Observe

Act

Teachers connect theory and practice...

Interpret

Plan change

• Reflect on the
  observations to try to
  understand why things
  are happening as
  they are.
  – What is working well?
    What are the factors
    that seem to make this
    possible?
  – What is not working
    well? What are the
    factors that need
    adjustment?

• Put the planned
  change into
  action.

• Analyse the factors to identify
  changes that would likely
  bring about an improvement.

• Select one or more of these
  changes that can feasibly be
  undertaken and plan how to
  carry it out.

Adapted from Wells, G. *Changing Schools From Within: Creating Communities of Inquiry*. Portsmouth,
NH: Heinemann, 1994.

Pre-service and In-service Programs

Teachers in pre-service, in-service, or special qualifications course settings may gain insight from a study of the literacy and second language practices in this resource, although it is not intended to stand alone as a manual of FSL methodology.

Professional Learning on a Continuum

FSL students learn best in learning environments that support risk taking and engagement—so do teachers! In whichever manner you approach this resource in order to make it meaningful for yourself, we encourage you to consider your professional learning on a continuum that is ever evolving given your experiences, language and comfort level, and the shifting needs of your students.

Professional Learning Tools

As an FSL teacher, you may self-assess your strengths at the outset of your engagement with this resource, and think about your professional growth along the way. A Professional Learning Survey is provided as a starting point for you to consider where you are in the development of your teaching skills with regards to the following:

- engaging and motivating students;

- integrating oral language;

- developing language awareness;

- assessing and differentiating;

- activating strategies.

Return to this inventory as you work through this resource and try the various strategies and tactics with your students. *On y va!*

Professional Learning Survey

Place a check mark in the appropriate column to assess your strengths as an FSL teacher at this time.

	Rarely	Sometimes	Frequently	Notes
1. Engaging and motivating students **a)** I make connections between FSL and students' interests, ideas, life experiences, and cultural background. **b)** I choose texts that are interesting and meaningful for students as a basis for real projects and tasks.				
2. Integrating oral language **a)** Oral language is at the centre of my instruction. Using French in the classroom is encouraged and validated. **b)** I provide authentic oral language models, which my students can adapt to reflect their personal experiences. **c)** I support my students' oral language development *before*, *during*, and *after* the exploration of aural, visual, and written texts.				
3. Developing language awareness **a)** I help students discover patterns using sound-symbol relationships, cognates, word families, and language structures. **b)** I support my students as they apply language patterns to express themselves in French.				
4. Assessing and differentiating **a)** I adjust my teaching before and during instruction to address the diverse learning needs of my students. **b)** I involve students in assessing and improving upon their own learning.				
5. Activating strategies **a)** I encourage my students to use strategies to help them "learn how to learn" in FSL. **b)** I help my students recognize connections between what they learn in FSL and what they learn in other subject areas.				

Setting the Context: Literacy in FSL

Introduction

Integrating literacy practices in French as a Second Language (FSL) teaching and learning is an effective way to motivate and engage students and to help them achieve success in French. Current research indicates that exploring a variety of aural, visual, and written texts leads to increased language proficiency in both students' first and second languages (Elley, 1991; Guthrie, 2004; Krashen, 2004). Students, teachers, administrators, and parents may all benefit from seeing more clearly how FSL contributes to and builds on students' literacy development, second-language learning, life skills, knowledge, and general education.

We have chosen to use the term "French as a Second Language" (FSL) in this resource to recognize the various contexts in which French is taught across Canada. Our primary audience is the professional community of French teachers who teach French as a subject area, in some cases called Core or Basic French in elementary FSL. The amount of time and intensity dedicated to FSL in these contexts vary from province to province. The general term FSL may also be used to refer to Immersion and Intensive French programs. What unifies all these contexts is the central concept that almost all elementary FSL students in Canadian schools today can develop literacy skills in first- and second-language learning.

How is Literacy Defined in FSL?

Literacy is an important educational concept around the world. However, there are many definitions used to define this complex concept. To understand literacy within the FSL context, the following definition proposed by the Ontario Ministry of Education is clear and useful:

> "Literacy is... the ability to use language and images in rich and varied forms to read, write, listen, speak, view, represent, and think critically about ideas. It enables us to share information, to interact with others, and to make meaning. Literacy is a complex process that involves building on prior knowledge, culture, and experiences in order to develop new knowledge and deeper understanding."
>
> *Ontario Ministry of Education, 2004*

This definition provides an excellent frame of reference for literacy in FSL, in part, because of the clear parallels it draws with the overall goals and outcomes of FSL curriculum documents from all Canadian provinces and territories and beyond (e.g., B.C. Ministry of Education, 2001; Atlantic Provinces Educational Foundation, 1996; Ontario Ministry of Education and Training, 1998). Though elementary FSL students are limited in their ability to articulate critical thinking in French, the goal of all FSL programs across Canada is to engage students with texts aimed at developing their abilities to listen, speak, read, write, view, and represent in French. In addition, all programs promote a communicative-experiential approach to language learning in which interacting with others, making meaning, and sharing information are important. FSL programs across Canada, therefore, already promote literacy instruction.

When FSL students develop literacy skills in French, they become not only stronger literate learners in French, but also in English and in other languages. The FSL teacher plays a key role in helping students understand that the FSL classroom is indeed part of their literacy environment. In fact, FSL teachers *are* literacy teachers just like their colleagues in first language programs; many are already integrating literacy practices in their classes and developing students' literacy strategies. In some cases, these teachers may not feel conversant with literacy concepts used by their colleagues; this resource provides them with the literacy vocabulary and describes the concepts in FSL terms.

As a literacy teacher, the FSL teacher plays many roles in the classroom: organizer, facilitator, motivator, guide, information source, and language model. This resource provides many concrete examples of techniques that allow teachers to recognize the literacy practices they are already using. It also allows them to integrate additional literacy teaching into their FSL classes as they engage students with a variety of meaningful, age-appropriate, culturally relevant, and cognitively challenging texts.

What is a Literate FSL Student?

A literate FSL student does more than interpret and understand words when he or she interacts with a text, or tries to communicate in any language including in their second or additional language. Allan Luke and Peter Freebody (1990) propose a useful model to describe the four roles of the literate student. This model was developed in a first-language context, but can be modified and applied in FSL for many reasons (see page 20, Figure 2). Although learning a second language is similar in many ways to first-language learning, there are also differences that impact literacy development.

Many elementary FSL students are already literate in at least one other language. This previous language learning experience is advantageous for students who already know how to decipher the alphabet, understand how letters combine to make words, and how words work together in structures to express meaning in sentences. These students normally have developed literacy skills that they can transfer to French. In addition, elementary FSL students can generally grasp and communicate somewhat complex ideas in

For more on the role of the FSL literacy teacher, see Big Idea 1, p. 34.

While there are many similarities between L1 and L2 learning, the variation in situation and other factors also produces many differences. One difficulty is filtering out differences that are accidental rather than inevitable. L1 children mostly acquire language in different settings with different exposure to language than L2 learners and they are at different stages of mental and social maturity.

(Cook, 2000)

For more on transfer between first, second, and additional languages, see Big Idea 5, p. 64.

their first language. We believe it is crucial for FSL teachers to make explicit connections to students' literacy skills in their first language, which they can activate and transfer to French class.

However, elementary FSL students do not have the vocabulary base, or understanding of how the French language works, to allow them to function at the same cognitive level as in their first language. Moreover, FSL is generally offered in short, non-intensive blocks of time. These challenges underline the importance for teachers to activate students' prior knowledge of, and experiences with, the themes and content that they develop in French class.

Despite the challenges of the FSL context, the Luke and Freebody model is a useful way to understand what a literate FSL student does to understand texts of all kinds. When FSL students encounter meaningful, age-appropriate, culturally relevant, and cognitively challenging texts at their linguistic level, they break the code in these texts and do much more than just focus on words and structures. However, in order to communicate effectively, students must also make meaning or sense of these texts; they must use these texts for concrete and real purposes. Students must analyse and critique them within the constraints of time and intensity, and their age and developmental level.

For more on breaking the code, see Big Idea 3, p. 47.

> Any program of instruction in literacy, whether it be in kindergarten, in adult second language classes, in university courses, or any points in between, needs to confront these roles (i.e., the four roles of the literate learner in FSL) systematically, explicitly, and at all developmental points.
>
> *(Freebody, 1992)*

Figure 2

The Four Roles of the Literate FSL Learner

Text User
- Students use engaging, relevant texts to communicate authentic aural, visual, and written messages in French.

Meaning Maker
- Students draw on prior knowledge and experiences to understand in their first and second language, to make sense of texts, and to communicate a real and relevant message when listening, speaking, reading, writing, viewing, and representing.

The FSL Learner

Text Analyser and Critic
- Students provide global responses to the content in texts and the emotions these texts evoke. They provide opinions and infer meanings from visual or graphic texts.

Code Breaker
- In aural and audiovisual texts, students focus on tone of voice, intonation, facial expression, body language, images, and cognates.
- In written text, students examine text format and organization, graphics and visuals, spelling, words, and language structures they already know.
- Students transfer code-breaking skills from their first language to make sense of sounds and symbols, words, and language structures that they do not already know.

Adapted from Freebody, P. "A Socio-Cultural Approach: Resourcing Four Roles as a Literacy Learner." In Watson, A. and Badenhop, A. (Eds.). *Prevention of Reading Failure*. Gosford: Ashton Scholastic, 1992.

Literacy Strategies Linking First- and Second-Language Learning

Research evidence shows how students who develop literacy skills in their second language are able to transfer these skills to their first language, and vice versa. Turnbull (1999) shows, for example, how Grade 9 Core or Basic French students engaged in a project-based and text-rich teaching approach outperform those who don't.

Admittedly, research in elementary FSL contexts is limited. However, research from other FSL contexts is relevant and has implications for elementary FSL. French immersion students learn foundational literacy skills in French before English instruction begins at school. These students successfully transfer these strategies when they use text and communicate in their first language (Swain et al., 1990; Turnbull, Lapkin, and Hart, 2001).

Similarly, students from Intensive French programs (Germain and Netten, 2004; Carr, 2007) spend one intensive school semester in French while the regular English curriculum is compacted into the second semester. Research shows that the literacy strategies these students develop in French are successfully transferred to English and to other school subjects taught in English. Regular Core or Basic French programs that have been modified as a follow-up for these intensive programs also include explicit literacy instruction. These students successfully develop literacy skills in French, which they transfer to English and other school subjects.

> "The effect of learning a second language (e.g., French) on first language skills has been virtually positive in all studies. Although most studies on the effect of second language learning on first language literacy have been done in the area of French immersion education, one can also apply the findings to Core French and Intensive French programmes."
>
> *(Bournot-Trites and Tellowitz, 2002)*

Research about "how learners learn best" also influences what we know about the potential of second-language learning to contribute to effective literacy development in general. In their recent book entitled *Literacy, Technology and Diversity: Teaching for Success in Changing Times*, Cummins, Sayers, and Brown (2007) draw upon Bransford's research to affirm that learning is greatly enabled when several key principles are followed. Bransford and colleagues emphasize three conditions for effective learning: engaging prior understandings, integrating factual knowledge into existing frameworks, and taking active control over the learning process. A fourth principle, which is equally important, involves learning in a supportive community.

These key principles of learning are reflected in recent educational practices around language and literacy in both English and French first-language settings in Canada. These same educational practices could be useful in second-language contexts such as FSL. The table on the following page (Figure 3) considers how these principles may be applied, keeping in mind the limitations of time and intensity imposed on FSL programs.

Figure 3

Principles of Learning: Second-language Literacy

Students learn best when they...	Second-language students...
• **engage prior understandings.**	• make connections between the text and their personal identities and background knowledge. • build on prior knowledge so that they can identify what they "need to know." • learn new information in context. • acquire and practise vocabulary and basic structures in order to access texts. • make connections between their own language and other languages.
• **integrate factual knowledge into existing frameworks.**	• seek out patterns and connections. • follow a model and practise with teacher coaching. • break new content into manageable chunks, and process one chunk at a time. • read for overall comprehension, not for word by word understanding.
• **gradually, with scaffolding, take control of the learning process.**	• gradually become more autonomous in their learning. • apply key comprehension strategies. • become aware of language patterns in order to apply them to new situations. • talk about learning processes along the way. • use critical literacy skills, albeit in a limited way, depending on their language level. • generate new meanings and texts, and represent them in a variety of ways. • take ownership of their learning as they complete projects or tasks. • track their progress in the language through a portfolio or learning log. • reflect on learning. • self-assess to set further language learning goals.
• **participate in supportive communities.**	• follow a model and practise with a partner or in trios with teacher guidance. • work in pairs or groups on authentic tasks. • share new knowledge and demonstrate language learning to a real audience. • interact in a meaningful way with people who speak the target language. • take risks with the language in order to express meaning. • learn to ask questions and seek clarification to assist with meaning-making. • learn to self-monitor and self-correct. • develop an awareness of the relationship between a language and the cultures of those who live in the language.

For more on scaffolding, see Big Idea 2, p. 38.

For more on assessment opportunities, see Big Idea 4, p. 55.

Additional Benefits of Literacy Instruction in FSL

Learning a Language: Another Form of Literacy

Learning another language opens many doors. Those who believe that literacy extends beyond text-based literacy in the dominant language consider that learning an additional language means developing a new form of literacy—another bonus for students!

The concept of multiliteracies, a term first coined by a group of international scholars who formed the New London Group (1996), recognizes and validates the multilingual practices of citizens around the world. Multilingual citizens are more literate and better prepared than unilingual citizens to make sense of and communicate the variety of culturally specific forms of literacy available in complex pluralistic societies, such as those found in North America (Genesee and Cloud, 1998).

Organizations across Canada and around the world promote the cognitive, social, emotional, and economic benefits of learning an additional language. By promoting FSL education and helping students develop literacy strategies, we are empowering FSL students to become stronger multilingual citizens of the world. In addition, learning French in Canada equips students to communicate with Francophone Canadians within their own country and with the over 300 million French speakers around the world. Learning French and learning about Francophones promotes an awareness of linguistic and cultural diversity, essential for full participation in today's bilingual and multicultural Canada, and throughout the world.

> "...there is a value-added benefit of not only developing a second (or third) language but also building cross-cultural skills at no cost to other educational goals."
>
> *(Genesee and Cloud, 1998)*

For 700 reasons to study another language, refer to this Web site: <www.pearson professionallearning.ca>.

Information, Communication, and Multimedia Technologies: Multimodal Literacy

The concept of multiliteracies also highlights the relevance and importance of helping students engage with texts associated with information, communication, and multimedia technologies (e.g., electronic text messages and Web sites, simple Web blogs, e-mail, PowerPoint®, and texts made using mind-mapping software like Inspiration® and Smart Ideas®). This resource promotes literacy instruction in FSL that engages students in a multimodal way—that is, literacy instruction that helps students make sense of texts produced in a variety of modes: aural, audiovisual texts; electronic, artistic and graphic texts; and written texts. This multimodal approach will help students function, in French and in their first language, as well as in a globalized, technologically sophisticated, and knowledge-based society.

In Summary...

- Implementing literacy practices in junior FSL programs is both feasible and desirable.

- Integrating a literacy focus in FSL constitutes added value for students' overall education.

Professional Learning Survey

A. Consider using a learning log to explore and track your professional learning at several points in time—*before*, *during*, or *after* reading this section.

1. How would you define literacy in your own words? Draw on your previous classroom and life experiences, professional development, and knowledge.

2. Refer to the principles of learning on page 22, Figure 3. How do you *already* help students...

   a) engage prior understandings?

   b) integrate factual knowledge into existing frameworks?

   c) gradually, with scaffolding, take control of the learning process?

   d) learn as part of a supportive community in the classroom?

3. Can you think of examples of how learning French helps students with their first language? To what degree does learning other languages help students with their first language?

4. How do you communicate the benefits of learning French and other languages to your students? to their parents? to your colleagues?

5. What would you like to know about literacy in FSL?

B. Assess your comfort and familiarity with literacy concepts and vocabulary by shading the following continuum.

Date	1 Very comfortable and familiar	2 Somewhat comfortable and familiar	3 Somewhat uncomfortable and unfamiliar	4 Totally uncomfortable and unfamiliar	5 Not sure

Engaging and Motivating Students: Making It Real

- Students learn to communicate in a second language when they are engaged and motivated by meaningful, age-appropriate, culturally relevant, and cognitively challenging tasks and projects.

- A variety of oral, visual, and written texts serve as a springboard for meaningful, age-appropriate, and cognitively demanding tasks and projects.

Introduction

French as a Second Language (FSL) is an integral part of schooling for a large majority of young Canadians. Our experiences in elementary FSL have usually been positive—students are keen and eager to learn a new language! We hope to build on that enthusiasm in this document. We will share our ideas for engaging and motivating students by using meaningful, age-appropriate, culturally relevant, and cognitively challenging tasks and projects that make connections to the world of literacy.

As FSL teachers, we recognize that motivation is a key element of the learning process, and that effective learning stems from our ability to engage students in relevant activities. However, we cannot deny that many FSL students are not always as engaged and motivated as we want them to be. In fact, many students tell us (e.g., Atlantic Provinces Education Foundation, 2003) that FSL learning can be boring, repetitive, and disconnected from their interests and the real world. Further, students are sometimes unmotivated to study French because they believe that they do not achieve success in the language; many feel that they cannot understand or speak French after several years in the program.

We believe that this does not have to be the case. Examining the ways in which second language learners achieve success provides us with insights into how we can engage and motivate *all* learners to develop fluency and literacy in French.

> It is universally accepted that motivation plays a vital role in academic learning in general, and this is particularly true of the sustained process of mastering an L2 (a second language).
>
> *(Dörnyei, 2001)*

How do Second Language Students Learn Best?

Researchers, such as Gardner, Lalonde, and Moorcroft (1985); and Dörnyei (2001), have shown clear links between students' motivation, engagement, and their success in a second language. Student engagement—the commitment to learn French—often leads to increased motivation (i.e., a desire, need, or willingness to learn French) and greater success. Likewise, greater success can lead to greater engagement and greater motivation. The following diagram shows these relationships in a simple way.

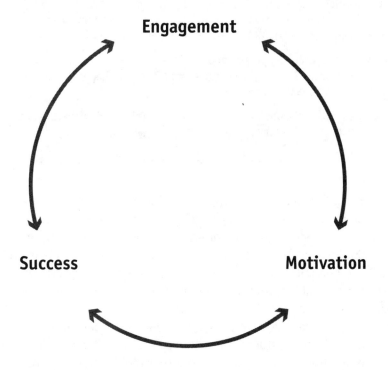

However, teachers know from experience that engaging and motivating students with authentic texts and tasks of all sorts in elementary FSL is far from simple. Their experience also indicates that integrating literacy strategy instruction into FSL makes sense, because doing so corresponds to how young students learn best. Bransford and colleagues (2000) from the cognitive psychology world suggest that engagement, motivation, and deep understanding in a learning context are best created when...

- instruction builds on students' prior learning and knowledge;

- students have the opportunity to learn with understanding;

- students are able to have control over the learning process.

A focus on developing strategies that will help students understand, talk, and write about texts that are authentic, interesting, challenging, age-appropriate yet linguistically accessible, will undoubtedly lead to increased engagement, motivation, and success in FSL.

For more on the Principles of Learning, see Setting the Context, p. 22.

Using Text as a Powerful Springboard for Real Tasks and Projects

Text refers to more than books—although books, big and small, are important. FSL teachers can use some of the following types of texts:

> **Aural:** students' oral presentations, simple radio ads and jingles, songs
>
> **Audiovisual:** video and film, video games, short film trailers (with little language), television advertisements targeted at young children
>
> **Electronic:** electronic text messages and Web sites, simple Web blogs, e-mail, multimedia presentations (e.g., PowerPoint®), texts made using mind-mapping software like Inspiration® and SMART Ideas™
>
> **Artistic and graphic:** picture books, visual art that incorporates words and images, signs, packaging, charts and graphs, maps, diagrams, illustrated word walls, and mind maps
>
> **Written:** lyrics of popular songs, poetry, accordion style novels, magazines, graphic novels, newspapers, and print advertisements

> "Extensive reading is critical to the development of reading proficiency. Extensive practice provides the opportunity for students to consolidate the skills and strategies teachers often work so hard to develop.
>
> *(Allington, 2002)*

Research (e.g., Allington, 2002; Krashen, 2004) indicates that students become more proficient listeners, speakers, readers, writers, and viewers of any language when they spend more time listening to, viewing, and reading texts as opposed to engaging in less communicative tasks, such as drill worksheets, non-authentic dialogues, or non-interactive games. This implies that students should frequently listen to, talk about, read, and view a variety of texts. These texts should not only come from several sources, but cover a variety of topics that are of interest to students and relevant to their real-life experiences. The more students are exposed to such texts, the more they will recognize that French can be used as another tool for thinking about their lives; and the more they use French to analyse, discuss, and reflect upon these texts, the more they will learn French. It is highly likely that students will be more motivated to do so because the texts respect their interests, learning styles, and learning histories.

Making connections to the literacy skills and strategies students already possess in their first language contributes to their literacy development in both languages (Cummins, 1981). However, teachers must help FSL students realize that they can transfer these strategies to learning a second language. In addition, involving students in the learning process through active engagement in meaningful, age-appropriate, and cognitively demanding tasks and projects, *in French*, is key to engaging and motivating FSL students. Varied aural, visual, and written texts, as listed above, serve as a springboard for these tasks.

> "Cognitive challenge and engagement are created by projects that "ignite" curiosity, imagination, and social commitment.
>
> *(Cummins et al., 2007)*

Teachers have found that the most effective and cognitively challenging projects (CASLT, 1994; Fried-Booth, 1986; Legutke and Thomas, 1991) relate to what elementary FSL students do in real-life. Topics or themes that are interesting and that matter to elementary students drive these projects, and are the focal point and defining characteristic of a communicative and experiential teaching approach that is common to all FSL programs across

Canada (CASLT, 1994; Tremblay et al., 1990). Projects should involve real inquiry, affirm students' identities and interests, and involve multimedia technologies.

An e-mail exchange between two elementary FSL classes is one example of a real, meaningful, and cognitively challenging project. In preparation to write e-mail messages to new friends in another part of the country or the world, teachers expose students to some real e-mail texts as models. They may teach them a strategy to understand these texts and then encourage students to create their own messages to be sent to real recipients.

Another such example might involve students reading and evaluating picture books and big books that are suitable for beginning FSL buddies. Students would share their assessment of the books, practise reading one text, and then actually meet a buddy with whom to read.

The Student at the Centre of the Learning Process

In project-based learning, engagement, cognitive challenge, and motivation are promoted by putting students' identities, emotions, needs, and interests front and centre. Students engage more in learning when they have a certain degree of choice and an opportunity to express preferences for the themes and activities in FSL learning. Being involved in controlling the learning process puts students at the centre of the learning, and is critical in developing their engagement, motivation, and success.

As teachers, we have also found that getting to know our students, showing an interest in their well-being, and showing them that their interests and needs count are all key to student engagement, motivation, and success. Moreover, project-based learning in FSL, which includes using texts to develop students' literacy strategies, must occur within a classroom environment that is welcoming, safe, encouraging, and supportive. (See p. 34.)

> "Dewey's idea of Project-based Learning (PBL) was introduced into the field of second-language education nearly two decades ago as a way to reflect the principles of student-centered teaching. Since then, PBL has also become a popular language and literacy activity at various levels and in various contexts.
>
> *(Hedge, 1993)*

Overview

Choosing the Right Texts

Choosing the right texts in FSL, when students' vocabulary is limited, is challenging. From experience, teachers find it difficult to engage and motivate students when using texts that do not relate to their interests, and which are not in line with their linguistic and cognitive development and maturity. Students are motivated to learn when they encounter interesting and meaningful texts on topics that matter to them.

We draw on Vygotsky's (1962) concept of the Zone of Proximal Development, which is a zone or gap between what learners cannot do alone but can complete successfully with the assistance or scaffolding of a more knowledgeable partner. According to Vygotsky's theory, incomprehensible text is text that is too many zones above the learner's level, regardless of the learner's metacognitive abilities, language and literacy skills, and strategies. The following criteria, based on research (e.g., Van Duzer, 1999) and extensive classroom experience, will help teachers select meaningful,

For more on scaffolding, see Big Idea 2, p. 38.

age-appropriate, cognitively challenging yet readable texts that also push students forward in FSL. The tables contrast characteristics of ideal versus less than ideal texts of various materials (aural, audiovisual, electronic, artistic and graphic, or written), keeping elementary FSL students and the classroom context in mind.

Figure 4

Criteria for Choosing Various Types of Texts

Aural and Audiovisual Texts

Ideal characteristics	Texts to avoid
• Texts contain little background noise, one or two different voices and clear, slow speech (yet not so slow that students know it's artificial). • Texts include voices of male and female persons, native Francophones, and learners of French.	• Texts contain intrusive background music or noise. • Texts include several speakers with similar sounding voices who do not identify themselves when speaking.

Electronic, Artistic and Graphic Texts

Real and relevant texts	Less real and less relevant texts
• E-mail messages written by peers	• An oral recording of an adult's e-mail message
• A graphic novel about weird and interesting festivities	• A graphic novel about traditional adult cultural activities
• A song from the 21st century that is popular with young people	• A song that is unpopular with or unknown to young people
• Youth graffiti	• A large and dark painting from the Middle Ages
• A trailer for a current movie that is popular with young people	• A trailer for a movie that is unpopular with or unknown to young people

Written Texts

Ideal characteristics	Less than ideal characteristics
• Language is simple, direct, economic (omission of needless words), and familiar (e.g., high frequency vocabulary).	• Texts contain uncommon vocabulary and complex, long sentences.
• Visuals are rich, attractive, abundant, and clearly convey meaning.	• Visuals are infrequent and do not clearly convey meaning.
• Texts are long enough to tell a story, or from which to gather information, but short enough to be accessible and readable.	• Texts do not convey much real meaning. • Texts are too long for the cognitive and linguistic development of students.
• Whole, authentic, real-life texts, which provide good examples of real discourse in French.	• Texts are chopped up and unnatural.
• Texts contain vocabulary, information, and concepts that are just beyond students' current abilities.	• Texts are simplistic and below students' cognitive and linguistic development. • Texts are too complex and well beyond students' cognitive and linguistic development.
• Texts include themes, situations, and characters that represent students' interests, experiences, and cultural backgrounds.	• Texts include themes, situations, and characters that are irrelevant to students. • Texts include culturally insensitive or biased scenarios.

Appendix A
See Checklist for Choosing Texts.

Choosing Texts that Connect to and Validate Students' Cultural Identities

Selon niveau...

Cummins et al. (2007) argue passionately and convincingly that literacy instruction should include texts and activities that connect to, and validate students' cultural backgrounds, leading to greater engagement, motivation, and success for these students. Moreover, the majority of language students will benefit from exposure to cultural perspectives that are different from their own, resulting in an increased appreciation for cultural diversity in a global community.

Connecting to and validating students' cultural backgrounds can include, but should not be limited to, food, festivals, and celebrations. Projects and texts should allow learners to reflect on and share family stories, experiences, and real everyday activities.

Implications for the Classroom

In this section, we draw on our personal experiences to propose practical strategies on how to use texts effectively within a project- or task-based teaching approach. We also provide ideas to ensure that students' cultural identities are linked to and validated in our use of texts in FSL.

Strategies to Identify a Purpose for Accessing Texts

Using texts of all types within task- or project-based teaching in FSL is key to engaging and motivating students (Knutson, 1997). Teachers must create a real purpose for listening to, viewing, reading, or speaking about these texts. The following strategies are helpful:

- Teachers create the context for an activity by identifying *why* they have chosen a particular text, *how* it relates to the project or task within a unit of study, *what* students will do when they access it, and what information they will glean from it.

- Teachers help students make connections to their lives and experiences by exploring students' prior experiences, which are related to the theme of the text, or by identifying how the task relates to what students have done before in their first language.

- Teachers model for students by talking about their own experiences related to the topic and/or task.

- Teachers ask students to identify the elements of the text that look or sound familiar.

EXAMPLE

In a learning sequence on nutritious foods, where the project or task is to prepare a recipe for a favourite nutritious dish and then create this dish, the following types of texts could be useful: images of different food types, Canada Food Guide, recipes, food labels, short restaurant TV ads advertising their specialties, student e-mails about their favourite foods.

Strategies for Connecting Students' Lives and Cultural Identities to the Content of Texts

- Teachers choose cultural, thematic content for texts and projects that reflects realities and experiences that validate students' diverse cultural identities.

- Teachers make cultural comparisons and encourage cultural sharing before, during, and after accessing texts.

- Teachers encourage students to identify cognates across languages.
- Teachers encourage students to create bilingual texts to share with peers and family members.

For more on cognates, see Big Idea 3, pp. 49–50.

> **EXAMPLE**
>
> In a learning sequence on nutritious foods, students from different cultural backgrounds could be asked to…
>
> - bring in recipes from home in their first language;
> - share favourite foods from home;
> - display food labels of foods from different countries;
> - talk about and compare meal traditions in their families.

Creating a Safe and Supportive Literacy Environment in FSL

Project- and task-based learning that incorporates meaningful and accessible texts of all kinds is challenging in FSL and must occur within a welcoming, safe, encouraging, and supportive environment. If students do not feel safe in the French classroom, they will shut down or misbehave, and will not demonstrate the engagement and motivation to learn French.

The chart on the following page, Figure 5, provides some practical ideas for setting up a safe, encouraging, and supportive literacy environment in the FSL classroom. These ideas are adapted from Jeroski (2007) to reflect the realities of most FSL classrooms.

> **In Summary…**
>
> - Students learn best when they are engaged and motivated.
> - Engagement and motivation are enhanced when students are involved in meaningful, age-appropriate, culturally relevant, and cognitively challenging tasks and projects.
> - Aural, visual, and written texts add real and meaningful dimensions to tasks and projects.
> - Students are most successful when they have input into the learning process in a safe and supportive environment.

Figure 5

FSL Literacy Teachers...

Focus on the student. They...

- establish routines that clearly articulate expectations.
- ensure students understand their role in the classroom. Direct movement between activities using planning boards or charts.
- ensure students have a say in what is presented on bulletin-board displays. Student participation helps to maintain interest, motivate learning, and stimulate inquiry.
- organize students to work in small groups, with partners, or independently. Make groupings flexible and change them to meet the demands of the learning task and the learner.

Create a positive classroom climate. They...

- get to know students' names as fast as possible.
- encourage risk taking for everyone in the class, including the teacher.
- provide ongoing constructive and encouraging feedback.
- avoid focusing too much on student errors in elementary FSL; focus only on the major errors and structures that are key to what is being taught.
- share *their* likes, dislikes, opinions, and life experiences.
- validate student success. Tell them they are doing well!

Use physical space to full advantage. They...

- arrange desks in a circle or in pods to promote pair and group work.
- use small groupings of desks or tables for hands-on activities, partner work, or student-teacher conferencing.
- section off a quiet area for independent listening, viewing, and reading.
- use an author's chair for presentations by individual students and for shared reading with students.
- provide activity centres that are purposeful and open-ended, and are not all pencil-paper tasks. Include criteria or a rubric for the task, and provide the needed resources (or ensure students know where to access them).

Use resource materials to full advantage. They...

- post Word Walls / Vocabulary Charts, Anchor Charts, and posters that outline literacy strategies and guide students as they work in French.
- make current reference materials (such as dictionaries, globes, atlases, handbooks, Internet, and schedules) an integral part of learning.
- provide a listening centre with CD player and computers.
- organize book bins or a class library containing large numbers of different sorts of texts.

Cultivate a cooperative approach with classroom teachers. They...

- negotiate space in the classroom for French supplies, bulletin board displays, displays of student work, or a quiet corner for a reading or listening centre.
- plan with the classroom teacher to include French in daily activities, for example, a French text could be sent home for reading with family members.
- discuss and negotiate clear routines and behaviour management strategies with the classroom teacher—students benefit from consistency!
- work with the classroom teacher to integrate literacy activities in the FSL class with the English program, and vice versa.
- provide regular updates on French classroom activities at staff meetings.

Professional Learning Survey

A. Consider using a learning log to explore and track your professional learning at several points in time—before or after reading this module, or while trying out an idea.

1. How do I make connections with and validate students in my FSL class? To what degree are their interests, ideas, life experiences, and cultural backgrounds at the centre of my FSL teaching?

2. What types of projects or tasks do I initiate with my FSL students? To what degree are these projects real and meaningful, age-appropriate, and cognitively challenging?

3. For what purposes do I use aural, visual, and written texts in my FSL classroom? To what degree do I use texts to encourage real learning—over and above learning the language?

4. What types of texts do I use for project- or task-based learning? How do students react to them? How linguistically appropriate are these texts? How real, interesting, and meaningful are they for my students and for myself?

5. How do I create a literacy environment in my FSL classroom—an environment where students are engaged and motivated to learn? How have I been successful? Which areas still need work?

B. What are your professional learning goals at this time?

1. I would like to advance my knowledge and understanding of…

2. I would like to try the following ideas from this module with the goal to…

C. Indicate your professional growth at this time by shading the following continuum, where 1 represents the beginning of your experimentation and 5 represents significant progress.

1. I choose texts that are linguistically appropriate yet cognitively challenging, and connect with students' interests, ideas, life experiences, and cultural background.

Date	1	2	3	4	5

Integrating Oral Language: Communicating for Success

- Various forms of text (aural, visual, and written) provide powerful starting points for students to interact with meaningful ideas in French. Teachers facilitate and support students' ability to access this content and interact with others by integrating authentic oral language use.

- Oral language use is integrated into the modes of listening, speaking, reading, writing, viewing, and representing; these modes are interdependent and reciprocal.

- Key comprehension strategies which facilitate meaning-making are explicitly taught and modelled by teachers, and practised by students with teacher support.

- Teachers develop students' language skills in their second language by supporting, modelling, and providing sufficient opportunities for shared and guided practice, until students can use these skills independently.

> Reading, writing, speaking, listening, viewing, and representing are closely interrelated. Experiences involving one or more language processes contribute to development in the others. As students develop strategies and proficiency in one aspect of language, they also improve in others.
>
> *(Jeroski, 2005)*

Introduction

The purpose of this module is to describe ways in which one of the language skills—oral language—can help further students' overall literacy development in their second language. We have chosen to focus on oral language because most students feel successful and motivated when they can express themselves orally in French. As teachers, we can help students develop oral language skills in French through the use of purposeful oral language.

Oral language skills are enhanced when French is used as much as possible to communicate with students in the FSL classroom. Some elementary FSL teachers speak mainly in French but use English occasionally, for example to debrief and reflect about learning or make cultural observations. Turnbull (2001) acknowledges that a judicious use of English can facilitate

effective literacy practices in **FSL: making connections**

understanding but emphasizes that teachers must make every effort to speak French in class given the limited amount of time usually available to second-language learning in most school systems.

Oral language can be integrated into the development of all the language skills. The four language skills—listening, speaking, reading, and writing—along with viewing and representing, are closely interrelated, and we can draw on these connections to help further students' literacy skills. Engaging elementary FSL students with aural, visual, and written texts of different types provides a language model as well as a stimulus for purposeful oral language use and discussion. For example, students can be encouraged to talk about their experiences with the topic by using simple language structures before exploring various types of text.

Why is Purposeful Oral Language Important?

FSL students develop the ability to communicate in French from the beginning of an FSL program through activities that are meaningful to them and connect to their lives; vocabulary and language structures are acquired as students use the language to communicate a real message. Students are motivated to learn the language because they can talk about aspects of their lives that interest them and see a purpose in using French. When students use language in meaningful, authentic contexts, they understand that they are using a real language for communication. In authentic contexts, the responses given by students in these activities are not prescribed. All these activities have a purpose beyond language, that is, beyond practising isolated vocabulary words.

> " Oral language is the foundation for development in reading and writing. "
>
> *(Fountas and Pinnell, 2001)*

EXAMPLES

- Students talk about their families.
- Students interview a classmate to discover what they are having for lunch. They could further classify the items according to the Canada Food Guide to reflect on healthy choices.
- Students talk to each other about what they enjoy as pastimes.

Overview

Exploring text can facilitate oral language development, expand vocabulary, develop comprehension skills, and provide stimuli for speaking, writing, and representing. There are numerous advantages for using text to stimulate and develop oral communication skills.

- Various forms of text provide a stimulus for oral communication by establishing a topic with which students have previous experience.
- Visuals included with text facilitate discussion and meaning-making.
- Text provides language models that students can use orally.
- Oral production of text improves pronunciation, enunciation, and intonation.

For more on modelling, shared practice, guided practice, and independent practice, see Comprehension Strategies, p. 73.

Gradual Release of Responsibility

In effective FSL instruction, teachers initially provide a lot of support to help students grow in their knowledge and use of the French language, but as students' proficiency grows, they are able to withdraw some of these supports. Known as scaffolding, this approach allows teachers to gradually release responsibility to students through the use of modelling, shared practice, guided practice, and independent practice. These are incremental steps that gradually build on students' skills and confidence until they no longer need teacher support and can work independently (Pearson and Gallagher, 1983). The following model demonstrates how teachers can apply scaffolding in the FSL classroom to develop students' independent use of oral language skills.

Figure 6

Dependence   Independence

To Learners	With Learners		By Learners
↓	↓		↓
Modelling	**Shared and Guided Practice**		**Independent Practice**
Modéliser	*Partager*	*Guider*	*Assimiler*
– *Moi, je le fais; vous, vous observez.*	– *Moi, je le fais; vous, vous m'aidez.*	– *Toi et ton ami(e), vous le faites; moi, je vous aide.*	– *Vous, vous le faites; moi, j'observe.*
The teacher models the language authentically while students observe and try to understand.	The teacher and students work together. The teacher models and helps students complete the activity.	Students are invited to complete the activity while the teacher helps them.	Students work independently by adapting the teacher's model as the teacher observes.

For example, in a simple interview, the teacher would say:
– *Je m'appelle...*
  J'aime le hockey.
	For example:
	– *Je m'appelle...*
	  Comment t'appelles-tu?
	– *J'aime le hockey. Quel sport est-ce que tu aimes?*
		For example, two students interview each other following the teacher's model while the teacher and classmates listen. The teacher helps them as needed, including correcting errors.	For example, students interview each other in pairs. The teacher observes and supports them by correcting errors, etc.

Adapted from: Pearson, P. and Gallagher, M. "The Instruction of Reading Comprehension." *Contemporary Educational Psychology*, 8 (1983).

The First Phase: Before a New Text is Explored

Teachers lead students through the steps of contextualization, personalization, and anticipation as they prepare to engage with a new text.

Contextualization

Before introducing a text, the teacher explains the purpose for exploring the text as well as the type of text they will be listening to, viewing, or reading. For example, a song about sports could be introduced in a learning sequence in which students share their favourite sport, or a small book about amazing collections could be introduced in a learning sequence in which students talk about their own collections.

Personalization

Once the purpose is explained and the context for learning is established, students can make connections to the theme or topic by talking about their personal experiences. Teachers can first relate their own experiences about the topic, then ask students questions to get them to talk about their connections to the theme or topic and their life experiences. For example, if the text is about music, teachers may share that they like rock music and then ask students to share their favourite genre of music. By doing so, they personalize it using new key vocabulary in context to prepare students to listen to, view, or read the text, and use this language orally. This enables students to become familiar with new vocabulary through purposeful oral language use prior to exploring text.

> The pre-activity stage prepares students for the experience by helping them to anticipate what the activity will entail, activating their previous knowledge, and creating the context for learning.
>
> *(Tremblay, 1990)*

When students use language orally, teachers must be judicious in encouraging correct language use, that is, they should correct errors that impede comprehension while being sensitive to not over correct, which affects students' willingness to take risks with the language. To develop fluency, students should be asked to use the correction immediately in a complete sentence and have an opportunity to re-use it in various situations. As students develop fluency and accuracy, they begin to feel successful and are more willing to use the language.

Anticipation

After using some of the key language from the text orally and authentically, students are ready to anticipate what they are going to learn about by looking at the title and visuals of the text. They make predictions based on the clues about the topic and language they have identified. This serves to motivate students and get them interested in both the topic and the text. They will be more successful at comprehending if they have an opportunity to anticipate content beforehand. Teachers can use a Think Aloud at this time to demonstrate the thought processes involved in making their predictions.

The Second Phase: During the Exploration of a Text

During the process of exploring text, it is crucial that teachers ask questions to assess student comprehension. Although the initial questions should focus on students' knowledge and comprehension of the text, teachers are encouraged to ask questions that are in-line with the upper levels of Bloom's taxonomy as students become more proficient with the texts and with the language. The following are examples of questions that may be asked when students are listening to a song during a lesson sequence on clothing:

Bloom's Taxonomy and Examples for the FSL Classroom

> Knowledge: recall facts
> – *Qu'est-ce que c'est?*
>
> Understanding: classify, give examples, draw a picture
> – *Dans quelle saison est-ce qu'on porte ces vêtements? Classifiez les vêtements.*
>
> Application: graph, practice
> – *Qu'est-ce que les élèves portent aujourd'hui? Faites un graphique.*
>
> Analysis: compare and contrast
> – *Comparez vos vêtements en été et en hiver. Utilisez un diagramme de Venn.*
>
> Synthesis: make predictions, draw conclusions
> – *C'est l'hiver. Selon vous, qu'est-ce que Luc porte?*
>
> Evaluation: give opinions
> – *Est-ce que cette chanson est triste? Agréable? Drôle?*
> – *Quelle est ton opinion?*

> " Having a chance to talk about the story in process is especially great for second language learners. "
>
> *(Routman, 2003)*

Teachers should ask questions on the key points of the text using the illustrations and the text format for support. They explain to students what they feel are the key aspects and what clues they used to make their decisions. Students follow this model and, supported by teacher questioning, identify key elements and explain what clues they used to make their decisions. Throughout this cyclical process, students, with teacher support, will continue to predict, adjust by verifying their predictions, and predict again what will happen next to help them make meaning.

If the text is written, teachers may use various methods to read the text orally, such as demonstration, shared reading, and reading in unison. In shared reading, students see the text, listen to the text being read with fluency and expression, and then are invited to read along. Through teacher modelling and encouragement, students join with their peers to read a text collaboratively—this provides maximum support and sets them up for a feeling of success. If the text is aural or audiovisual (such as a video, a television ad, or a song), teachers can use similar methods as those suggested for written text. Students may dramatize a video or re-enact a television ad using a script, or they may sing a song several times, acting out key words as they sing.

Teachers model and guide students in all aspects of reading for comprehension, fluency, figuring out words, thinking, questioning, predicting, and rereading (Routman, 2003). Teachers also have an opportunity to make students aware of graphophonics (sound-symbol relationships) during this process, thus helping to improve pronunciation, enunciation, and intonation.

For more on graphophonics, see Big Idea 3, p. 48.

The Third Phase: After Exploring Text

Students have an opportunity to use information they have obtained through exploring text for other purposes, including speaking, writing, and representing, to demonstrate their comprehension and to respond personally to the text. These activities allow students to share reactions, revisit text to obtain additional information, establish connections between what they have read and their prior knowledge, as well as make connections to their own lives.

Teachers could begin by leading an oral discussion in which students share the most interesting aspects of the text. Teachers provide models by using simple language that students can reproduce and change to reflect their own experiences and lives. The teacher shares an aspect of the text with a student; the student is then asked to share by repeating the language structure used; and finally the student responds with his or her personal answer.

Implications for the Classroom

A goal of FSL teaching is to enable students to understand, read, write, as well as speak French, in real communication situations outside the classroom. As discussed earlier, purposeful oral language is key to teaching a second language and connects with all the other modes (listening, speaking, reading, writing, viewing, and representing).

Purposeful oral language helps students comprehend and express their ideas; for example, students may talk about visuals before listening to, viewing, or reading a text. As students explore the text, they share their understanding orally by answering questions and relating the content to their own experiences. When beginning written work, students can brainstorm ideas they want to share in their writing. The teacher and the class would then create a template that students could use to frame their response, but adapt to their individual proficiencies/ideas.

The use of purposeful oral language is integrated throughout the three phases of exploring text: *before*, *during*, and *after*.

Before a New Text is Explored

Teachers...	Students...
Contextualization	
• give students a reason for engaging with text, or have them determine this deductively.	• understand why they are listening to, viewing, or reading a text.
Personalization	
• model new key vocabulary by talking about their personal experiences with the topic. – *J'aime...* – *Je fais...*	• listen as the teacher shares personal experiences and think about what they would say to reflect their own experience.
• ask questions using visuals and key words to provide students with the opportunity to adapt the model to reflect their situations. – *Qu'est-ce que tu aimes?* – *Qu'est-ce que tu fais comme passe-temps?*	• practise new vocabulary in authentic oral communication situations by adapting the teacher's model. – *J'aime...* – *Je fais...*
• help students personalize vocabulary by providing the French word and article in a complete sentence when students suggest first-language words related to the topic.	• ask for unknown words needed to talk about their own experiences related to the topic. – *Comment dit-on en français?*
• support students by using a model as they communicate with a partner.	• practise using the new vocabulary in authentic oral communication situations with a partner. – *J'aime... Et toi?* – *Je fais... Et toi?*
Anticipation	
• encourage students to ask questions about the text, using headings and illustrations. – *Quel est le titre?* – *Quelles images est-ce que vous voyez?*	• ask simple questions about the text features to clarify their thinking about the text. – *Quel est le titre?* – *Quelles images est-ce que je vois?*
• use a Think Aloud strategy to show their thought process when making predictions.	• observe how the teacher makes predictions, and then make predictions in the same way.
• ask questions about what might happen to elicit predictions.	• make informed predictions based on what they already know about the text.
• model the use of graphic organizers (such as a Place Mat, a Fish Bone, or a K-W-L Plus Chart) to make connections to prior knowledge, ask questions, and predict content.	• use a graphic organizer to record prior knowledge and experience with the topic, ask questions about the topic, and predict the content of the text.

Appendix A
See Fish Bone, K-W-L and K-W-L Plus Charts, and Place Mat.

effective literacy practices in **FSL: making connections**

During the Exploration of a Text

Teachers...	Students...
• pause and ask questions to verify predictions and anticipate future content. • think aloud to point out what clues were used to verify predictions.	• check their understanding after each chunk of text. • create mental images in their minds about the text by visualizing. • verify predictions and make more predictions.
• model "monitor and repair" strategies to help students make meaning of the text.	• go back and listen to, view, or read a chunk of text more than once. • go back and check text features and visuals to decode meaning. • use a glossary or other resources to find the meaning of key words.

• provide graphic organizers (such as Flow Charts, Timelines, or Story Maps) to help students distinguish main ideas from details, and organize information as they explore text.	• use graphic organizers to:
	  – summarize information with simple sentences or images;
	  – sequence events or organize information from the text;
	  – determine important information.

• ask questions to raise awareness of graphophonic clues.	• recognize patterns and differences in words in written and oral text. • think of known words that resemble new words.
• create word walls or vocabulary banks with students organized by theme, sounds, symbols, etc. • use words in context.	• use word walls and vocabulary banks as references and tools for future listening, speaking, reading, writing, viewing, and representing.

• provide numerous opportunities for students to practise a text to develop fluency and accuracy:
  – shared or unison reading;
  – reader's theatre;
  – choral reading, etc.
	• practise the text several times using different methods.

• listen and model correct usage as students practise the text in groups.	• practise the text in groups, helping each other when needed.

Appendix A
See Flow Chart, Timeline, and Story Map.

Appendix A
See Word Wall/ Vocabulary Bank.

After Exploring the Text

Appendix A
See Venn Diagram.

Appendix A
See Retelling and Role Play, and Interview.

Teachers...	Students...
• help students see connections between the text and themselves, their world, and other texts using a graphic organizer (e,g., Venn Diagram).	• make links between the information in the text and their own experiences by comparing and contrasting using a graphic organizer (e.g., Venn Diagram).
• provide a choice of activities (oral, written, representing), which allows for personalization by students.	• transform information in the text into a new form. • orally demonstrate comprehension using a variety of activities, such as Retelling and Role Play, and Interviews.
• provide Sentence Starters and Anchor Charts to help students reflect on the text and demonstrate understanding.	• share reactions to the text with the whole class, or in small groups. – *J'aime…* – *Je n'aime pas…*

In Summary...

• Students prepare to explore text by:
  – accessing prior knowledge;
  – connecting personally to the topic;
  – using key vocabulary from the text orally in authentic communication situations;
  – making predictions.

• Students explore text by:
  – verifying their predictions;
  – checking comprehension;
  – reproducing the text by following a model.

• Students demonstrate comprehension of a text by:
  – connecting new knowledge to prior knowledge;
  – transforming information in a new form using various modes and mediums (speaking, writing, and representing).

Professional Learning Survey

A. Consider using a learning log to explore and track your professional learning at several points in time—before or after reading this module, or while trying out an idea.

1. How do I encourage oral language use in my FSL classroom? To what degree do I provide meaningful, authentic contexts for students to use oral language?

2. What do I do in my FSL classroom to provide authentic oral language models for my students? To what degree are students able to adapt models to reflect their personal experiences?

3. How do I help my students develop the necessary skills to speak independently? To what degree do I scaffold their learning by modelling and offering shared and guided practice?

4. What types of oral language activities do I provide *before*, *during,* and *after* listening to, viewing, or reading a text? To what degree do these activities succeed in helping students develop their oral language skills?

5. What types of opportunities do I provide for my students to use oral language when developing skills in all the modes (listening, speaking, reading, writing, viewing, and representing)? Which skill areas are the most well-developed? Which skill areas need the most work?

B. What are your professional learning goals at this time?

1. I would like to advance my knowledge and understanding of…

2. I would like to try the following ideas from this module with the goal to…

C. Indicate your professional growth at this time by shading the following continuum, where 1 represents the beginning of your experimentation and 5 represents significant progress.

1. I develop oral language use in authentic meaningful contexts integrating all modes of learning—listening, speaking, reading, writing, viewing, and representing.

Date		1	2	3	4	5

Developing Language Awareness: Discovering Patterns

- To learn a language, students must understand how the language code functions by developing knowledge and skills in phonics, spelling, grammar and sentence structure, and by recognizing patterns.

- Language structures are introduced to students as they need them and are able to use them to communicate. They are not a goal in and of themselves.

- Interest and motivation drive students' desire to use various tools to break the code and to understand oral and written language.

Introduction

> The world is a large and wonderful place; words help our students find their way in, through, and beyond the boundaries of their world, to the promise inherent in each.
>
> *(Beer, Probst, and Rief, 2007)*

As FSL teachers, we often love languages or have a vested interest in language learning, and have usually studied one or more languages ourselves. In our desire to pass on language knowledge to students, we sometimes lose sight of the reasons why we learned a second language in the first place. Among other reasons, we learned it to interact with French speakers, read and study French literature, enjoy French cinema, listen to French music, and travel in French-speaking countries.

Keeping the Focus on Language in Perspective

Language knowledge on its own, therefore, should not be the focus of FSL programs. Knowledge about how language works is a means to an end and not the ultimate goal. The goal in FSL teaching is to contribute to students' ability to communicate in French effectively by applying their knowledge of language *in context*. FSL students learn about how language works so that they can understand and use language, orally and in written form, for real and meaningful communicative purposes. Students show interest in learning verb forms, adjective endings, word derivations, and so on—insofar as this learning helps them understand aural, visual, and written text and use it to communicate their own idea.

effective literacy practices in **FSL: making connections**

In this module, we will explore several ways to help students discover patterns within words and in language that will contribute to their language awareness and help them better understand and communicate in French. Tools are introduced and ways to implement these tools in the classroom are suggested.

Overview

Language Forms, Language Awareness, and Breaking the Code

The following terms can best describe the role that language plays in the FSL classroom when the goal is comprehension of text and authentic communication.

Language forms is the term used to group together a number of different components of language, including grammar, phonics, sentence structure, and spelling patterns. Language awareness refers to students' capacity to understand how these language forms operate and how meaning is made. Breaking the code means using the skills and knowledge about language forms and language awareness to make sense of aural, visual, and written text. To do so, students use a variety of code-breaking tools, such as sound-symbol relationships, cognates and familiar words, word families, and language structures. Luke and Freebody (1990) view the student's capacity to break the code as one of the primary resources in the literate learner's toolkit.

Implications for the Classroom

Developing Students' Skills for Effective Decoding

FSL teachers help students develop language awareness and code-breaking skills by introducing them to some strategies and tools that will assist them, while remaining mindful of the following three principles:

- Learning how language works and using tools to engage students should be enjoyable for them.

- The tools should be appropriate to students' language level and be introduced in context—just-in-time for students to use them. This refers to introducing tools and providing information as students need them. For example, teaching students that the preposition *à* is always used with the name of a town or city is best taught when students need to say where they live.

- Extensive opportunities for practice in meaningful contexts will help students develop comfort and skill using these tools for real purposes.

Most students have an inquisitive nature. Discovering patterns and learning about how language works is an automatic extension of this innate curiosity. Students enjoy solving puzzles and can transfer some of the skills they are developing in math—problem solving, recognizing number patterns, completing a series of numbers—to some of the tools that can be used to understand how language works. Introducing tools for working with language

> " As code breakers, students...
> - become aware of and decipher features and language forms in texts.
> - focus on tone of voice, intonation, facial expression, body language, images, and cognates (in aural and visual texts).
> - examine text format and organization, graphics and visuals, spelling, words, and structures they already know (in written text).
> - transfer code-breaking skills from their first language to make sense of spelling, words, and structures that they do not already know in their second language. "
>
> *(Luke and Freebody, 1990)*

engages students and provides them with interesting and entertaining ways to explore and practise these strategies.

When students begin to see and understand patterns in language, they acquire very useful tools that help them understand how words work so that they can decode texts and produce their own oral and written language. As students explore patterns within words and sentences, they learn about general spelling patterns and increase their knowledge of the meaning of individual words. Students' general knowledge of word and sentence patterns helps them to decode new words and sentences that have recognizable patterns.

Considering the age level of students and the fact that they are beginning learners of FSL, teachers may focus on four key tools to help develop students' language awareness: sound-symbol relationships, cognates and familiar words, word families, and language structures.

Sound-symbol Relationships

> If teachers encourage children to investigate and puzzle out how sounds and letters work, then children are actively constructing knowledge and understanding about language.
>
> *(Hill, 2006)*

The focus of a beginning and intermediate FSL program is oral language, although all modes of learning are integrated early on. Students will have heard many of the words that they will see in written texts, but the written form may appear foreign to them. Texts with many unknown words may be intimidating to students. Providing opportunities for students to develop an understanding of sound-symbol relationships is a key building block in working with words.

The term graphophonics is used to refer to the relationship between symbols (the letters of the alphabet) and the sounds they make when pronounced. To explore this term, consider the following messages written by students to introduce themselves:

a.
Bonjour! Ici Tyler. Ma famille habite à Windsor en Nouvelle-Écosse. Je parle français et anglais. La nature est très belle dans les provinces maritimes. J'adore les pommes.

b.
Salut! Je m'appelle Lilyanne. J'habite à Canmore en Alberta. Je parle polonais et anglais, et j'apprends le français aussi. J'adore la randonnée dans les montagnes!

c.
Salut! Ici, Tomas. J'ai neuf ans. Ma famille habite à Old Crow au Yukon. Je parle tutchone, tchèque et anglais, et j'apprends le français. Voici l'aurore boréale. C'est beau, n'est-ce pas?

In the messages, second-language learners may already be familiar with the sound represented by the letters *–ais* in a word such as *français*. When students encounter words, such as *anglais* or *polonais*, they will recognize the same symbol *–ais* and be able to draw on the sound produced to pronounce these new words correctly. Similarly, students may recognize the pronunciation of the symbol *–au* in phrases that they hear and say often, such as *au revoir* or *il fait chaud*. Students will then recognize this same pattern in new words they do not yet know like *autres*, *au Yukon*, and *aurore boréale*.

It is precisely this sound-symbol relationship and the patterns that students perceive among common sounds and symbols that contribute to their capacity to successfully decode text.

There are a number of ways to help students see patterns and practise sound-symbol relationships. Word Sorts are activities that require students to group together words or parts of words with similar sounds. Word sorts can also be presented as images for concrete words or as oral activities. Consider the difference between the nasal –*u* as in *Salut!* and the open –*ou* as in *Nouvelle-Écosse*. Students can benefit from a Word Sort done as a class or in pairs, which gives them practice in differentiating between sounds in words that they are learning to produce. The words practised in these activities should always be words that students are presently learning so that they see them in a real text. They can also be taken from earlier projects or tasks done during the course of the year.

Appendix A
See Word Sorts.

Cognates and Familiar Words

Cognates are words that have a similar or identical form in two different languages and have the same meaning. (Otherwise, the two words are known as a *faux-amis*). As there are many English words that have a very similar form in French, students should be encouraged to rely on their knowledge of English or another language to help decode texts in French. Helping students to decode a text and derive meaning enhances student comprehension and independence. Some words are not necessarily cognates but simply familiar words that students already know, such as *un ami, bonjour, le français.* Helping students focus on familiar words and look for cognates will help reduce anxiety and contribute to their ability to successfully decode a text.

In a learning sequence on snacks, students listen to TV ads on food aimed at kids. While listening, they may encounter the following English cognates:

> *Ma collation préférée est la pizza. Sur ma pizza, je mets du pepperoni, des oignons, des tomates et du fromage. J'aime manger de la pizza au restaurant et à la maison.*

Although students may not have identified all of these words initially, they will develop their ability to detect cognates with additional practice. To assist students to develop this skill, encourage them to brainstorm a list of the words they hear or underline words in a text that resemble English words. Some words will be identical, such as *la pizza, du pepperoni,* and *le restaurant,* while others may have a slight variation in spelling or an accent, such as *des tomates.* Other cognates will be disguised a little more carefully, such as *des oignons.*

To help students recognize cognates, introduce them to common roots that many French words share with other languages. Encourage them to look for these roots and to talk about the languages they know. The word *scolaire*, for example, is linked to the English word *school* and the German word *Schule.* Ask students to provide a few examples of words that are similar in several different languages. This type of activity has the added benefit of affirming students' cultural identities and making more connections for additional language learners.

EXAMPLES

French	Italian	German	English	Tagalog
chocolat	*cioccolato*	*Schokolade*	chocolate	*tsokolate*
téléphone	*telefono*	*Telefon*	telephone	*telepono*
tigre	*tigre*	*Tiger*	tiger	*tigre*
chat	*gatto*	*Katze*	cat	*pusa*

A Word Wall or Word Web are useful tactics to help students recall some of the cognates and familiar words they have learned and will continue to recognize in texts. Various cognates may be printed on index cards and posted on the wall in categories associated with projects or tasks undertaken during the year. For example, the teacher may want to create a Word Wall for *la pizza* and *les collations* but later reorganize these same words on the Word Wall with students to highlight word families, and yet again to highlight a particular sound-symbol relationship. It is always essential that students learn and use words in context. As words are added to the Word Wall, students must be aware of their use and meaning in the context of an oral or written text.

Appendix A
See Word Wall/ Vocabulary Bank, and Word Web.

Word Families

Introducing students to word families is an excellent way to increase their active and passive vocabulary. Word families are groups of words that share a common root that links them together. For example, the verb *patiner* belongs to the same word family as *le patin, le patinage, le patineur, la patineuse,* and the words *le musicien* and *musical* are derivatives of the word *la musique*. In a learning sequence on sports, in which students listen to a video about Canadian sports heroes and talk about their favourite sports, teachers may present other verbs such as *patiner* that may be modified to form nouns such as *patineur*.

EXAMPLES

– *Qui aime **jouer** au basket-ball?*
– *Moi, j'aime jouer au basket-ball. Je joue bien.*
– *Eh toi, est-ce que tu es **un bon joueur** ou **une bonne joueuse** de basket-ball?*

– *Qui aime **skier**?*
– *Moi, j'aime skier.*
– *Est-ce que tu es **un skieur** avancé ou **une skieuse** avancée?*

– *Qui aime **nager**?*
– *Moi, j'aime nager.*
– *Eh toi, est-ce que tu es **un bon nageur** ou **une bonne nageuse**?*

Rather than directly teaching each individual vocabulary word to students, time will be better spent providing them with tools for problem solving and analysis. This will enable them to detect parts within new words that are familiar so that they can generate new vocabulary themselves.

Prefixes and suffixes can also be used to expand students' vocabulary. In daily instructions, teachers may point out that the suffix *re* plays the same role as it does in English and can be applied to a number of actions. In a learning sequence on families, in which students read about different types of families, students' ability to talk about their families is increased when they can take the verbs *aimer* and *adorer* and attach the suffix *–able* to create *aimable* and *adorable*. These new words, created from familiar words, expand students' vocabulary and give them a sense of achievement.

EXAMPLES

– *Je **lis** le texte encore une fois. Je **relis** le texte.*
– *Je **place** le crayon sur le pupitre encore une fois. Je **replace** le crayon sur le pupitre.*
– *Je **fais** le travail encore une fois. Je **refais** le travail.*

– *Tu **aimes** ta grand-mère. Elle est **aimable**, n'est-ce pas?*
– *Oui, elle est aimable.*
– *Tu **adores** ton chien. Il est **adorable**, n'est-ce pas?*
– *Oui, il est adorable.*

To help students explore word families, you may wish to create a Word Wall organized by word families by starting a column with a new word and then adding to this column additional words that are part of this family. For example, students may encounter the verb *courir* and later encounter the word *une course* that can be added to the wall.

Opportunities for students to develop their knowledge of word families can be found in all texts. Before exploring a particular text, teachers may identify patterns within the text that students are ready to manipulate and that would advance their oral language development. In this way, students hone their problem-solving skills while engaging in entertaining and enriching activities that enhance code-breaking skills and language awareness.

Language Structures

To avoid presenting grammar and language structures out of context, FSL teachers remain vigilant of just-in-time opportunities. For example, when students express what they like to do in a learning sequence on activities, teachers have an opportunity to orally introduce the verb *aimer* and teach students some forms of a regular *–er* verb: *j'aime, tu aimes, il aime, elle aime*.

It is important to note that the conjugation of an *–er* verb is not taught for its own sake, but because students need to know this language structure in order to communicate effectively.

> **EXAMPLE**
>
> – *Moi, **j'aime** la bicyclette. Et toi, Bakir?*
> – *J'aime le soccer.*
> – *Très bien. **Tu aimes** le soccer. Larissa, qu'est-ce que ton amie Amy aime?*
> – ***Elle aime** le soccer.*

Appendix A
See Language Games.

This introduction of a language structure gives students language they will need in order to talk about their own preferences and eventually to write about them. The teaching and the learning are contextualized and presented to help students meet a real and meaningful communicative goal: talking and writing about things they like.

> There is no one path to becoming literate but, rather, multiple paths... Literacy takes on shape, pattern, and texture as it is constructed to meet a range of purposes and functions.
>
> *(Hill, 2006)*

In Summary...

- The use of tools, such as sound-symbol relationships, cognates and familiar words, word families, and language structures offer opportunities for students to apply their prior knowledge and problem-solving skills to further develop their vocabulary and language awareness.

- Students cannot rely on simply memorizing vocabulary lists to help them understand aural, visual, and written texts. They must rely on their own knowledge about how language works to help them predict what new words might mean and how they are pronounced.

- It is important that teachers spend time providing students with opportunities to develop and practise these skills within real and meaningful contexts.

Professional Learning Survey

A. Consider using a learning log to explore and track your professional learning at several points in time—before or after reading this module, or while trying out an idea.

1. How do I help students discover language patterns as they listen to, view, and read texts? To what degree do I choose patterns in a given text that will advance students' overall language development?

2. How do I use sound-symbol relationships to help students recognize word patterns? To what degree does this tool help students produce language effectively?

3. How do I use cognates to help students recognize similarities between French, English, and other languages? To what degree does this tool increase students' comfort level with new text?

4. How do I use word families to help students recognize word patterns? To what degree does this tool help students increase their active and passive vocabulary?

5. What types of activities do I initiate in my FSL classroom to help students recognize patterns in language structures?

B. What are your professional learning goals at this time?

1. I would like to advance my knowledge and understanding of…

2. I would like to try the following ideas from this module with the goal to…

C. Indicate your professional growth at this time by shading the following continuum, where 1 represents the beginning of your experimentation and 5 represents significant progress.

1. I teach language patterns in context, when they are useful to students for real communication using aural, visual, and written texts.

Date		1	2	3	4	5

Assessing and Differentiating: Reaching All Learners

- Ongoing assessment strategies inform teaching and learning in the FSL classroom.

- Differentiation strategies that respond to students' diverse backgrounds, language proficiencies, and learning needs have a powerful impact on their engagement, learning, and self-esteem.

- Teachers use ongoing assessment strategies to scaffold and differentiate FSL learning contexts to address the diverse needs of students.

Introduction

Students of FSL, as in other subject areas, bring very diverse backgrounds, abilities, and attitudes to the learning environment. Being aware of this diversity, planning for it, and responding to varying needs along the way will help engage students in learning. In this module, we will explore practical ways of using assessment for learning (Stiggins, 2002) and differentiated instruction (Tomlinson, 2001) to ensure that as many students experience success as possible.

Assessment *for* Learning refers to the ongoing processes teachers use, formally and informally, to monitor students' progress with authentic tasks, adjust teaching based on this information, and involve students in understanding their own learning (Stiggins, 2002).

In FSL, the challenge of reaching all students is facilitated by using ongoing assessment tools and differentiation strategies hand in hand. Relevant and meaningful materials, appropriate expectations, the creation of a classroom climate that values risk taking and multiple intelligences (Gardner, 1993), and a degree of personalization and choice all contribute to higher student engagement, and more meaning-making in French.

> Positive assessment practices:
> - keep pedagogy at the centre—informing instruction.
> - develop capacity in teachers and students rather than externally controlling them.
>
> *(Cummins et al., 2006)*

What and *how* we can assess for learning and differentiate within the limits of the FSL classroom is governed by the following key principles:

- Ongoing assessment and differentiation is integral to all good teaching. Teachers assess at various stages of the learning process, using a variety of methods.

- Assessment *for* Learning provides meaningful information to both teachers and students, and helps students set goals for further learning.

- Students bring varying strengths and needs to the FSL experience. Groups of students may include: some who are multiliterate and hence are capable of contributing prior knowledge of language learning; others of above or below average intellectual ability; and those with specific learning disabilities.

- Differentiated instructional interventions are planned for during lesson preparations and learning sequences, and emerge along the way, necessitating further practice, reteaching, or variations to help meet the needs of certain groups of students.

Overview

Incorporating Assessment Opportunities into the FSL Classroom

Assessment opportunities that are embedded in the everyday work of students include:

- observing individual and small group work in progress;

- conferencing with students;

- giving descriptive feedback on performances;

- making comments in learning logs;

- interacting with students around portfolios;

- evaluating presentations according to agreed upon criteria.

Ongoing feedback is often shared and discussed with students, so that they may better understand their own learning, make their own adjustments, and set their own goals. For example, the teacher gauges the ability of students to produce a coherent message by observing the ease with which they interpret the messages they receive and are able to manipulate and personalize the meaning. The teacher does this by asking questions of individual students and partners as they work independently or in small groups.

Students learn best when they demonstrate their learning by completing authentic tasks. Tasks that allow for choice and differing expectations—depending on individual student needs and following clear models and standards—increase engagement and support success. Students can engage more fully in their own language learning processes through shared assessments and goal setting.

> **Assessment *for* Learning:**
> – Encourage, not discourage;
> – Build confidence, not anxiety;
> – Bring hope, not hopelessness;
> – Offer success, not frustration;
> – Trigger smiles, not tears.
>
> *(Stiggins, 2003)*

> Significant gains in student achievement can be attributed to the increased accuracy of assessments, more descriptive feedback and more student involvement.
>
> *(Black et al., 2004)*

For more on scaffolding, see Big Idea 2, p. 38.

Assessment *of* Learning (Stiggins, 2003) takes place when the teacher considers all the steps in the learning process, that is, the Assessment *for* Learning, as well as the quality of the end product or performance, to form a judgement about a student's learning at a certain point in time. The teacher's judgement, expressed with reference to commonly held expectations, becomes Assessment *of* Learning, or the evaluation component. These evaluation points, shared with students and parents, should also be used for setting further learning goals. For example, in a learning sequence where students exchange e-pal messages with another class, the students' ability to talk about their lives and experiences during and after instructional steps would be monitored by the students and the teacher in a learning log. Students and teacher would make observations and assessments of progress with the task and the end product, which may be shared with parents.

The crucial distinction between Assessment *of* Learning and Assessment *for* Learning lies in how the question is asked.

Assessment *of* Learning:	How much have students learned at a particular point in time?
Assessment *for* Learning:	How can we use ongoing information to help students learn more?

Stiggins, 2003

> In a differentiated classroom, the teacher proactively plans and carries out varied approaches to content, process, and product in anticipation and response to student differences in readiness, interest, and learning needs... A differentiated classroom is marked by a repeated rhythm of whole class preparation, review and sharing, followed by opportunity for individual and small group exploration, sense-making, extension, and production.
>
> *(Tomlinson, 2001)*

What is Differentiated Instruction in the FSL classroom?

Differentiated instruction refers to either pre-planned or mid-course interventions, adaptations, and teaching tactics that teachers introduce with individual students, flexible groups, or the whole class, to facilitate students' success (Tomlinson 2001). For example, students may encounter difficulty with a particular structure or pattern, which would require reteaching or more explanation. Vocabulary that is more personalized may need to be introduced to individuals and groups of students. Teachers plan for differentiation based on observing individual student and group readiness, interests, and abilities at the outset of a task or learning sequence. Teachers engage students by drawing on their backgrounds and providing them with the necessary language to share their experiences with others. For example, a teacher may ask students to identify cognates, the places where they have lived on a map, or list activities that interest them on a word wall.

Teachers are able to tailor instruction along the way by monitoring comprehension. They circulate during guided practice, small group, and partner work to monitor the ability of individual students to make meaning and provide models as necessary. For example, a teacher may stop and help partners in difficulty work through an independent activity by asking questions to guide them through the activity and provide a model as appropriate.

When, why, and *how* to incorporate Assessment *for* Learning and differentiated instruction in second-language learning sequences is illustrated by the following diagram:

Figure 7

Assessment and Differentiation Cycle

- Assess the performances of learning.
- Discuss strengths and areas of need with the whole class, groups, and individuals.
- Incorporate needs into future learning sequences.
- Begin again!

- **Plan initially for degrees of difficulty, groupings, choice, and personalization based on prior knowledge of students' needs.**
- **Adapt for the more or less able learners.**

- Differentiate based on the nature of the students in a class.

- **Provide models/sentence starters for student performances of their learning.**
- **Engage students in observations of others, and in self-assessment.**

FSL Teaching/Learning

- **Introduce the purpose of the learning sequence.**
- **Assess prior knowledge for the topic and activate connections.**
- **Develop criteria for success.**
- **Provide concrete examples to model student outcomes.**

- **Engage students in meaning-making with the text.**
- **Provide graphic organizers and individual, partner, and small group practice for manipulating the language in the text.**
- **Use a variety of manipulative and kinesthetic activities.**
- **Assess individual and overall success with each task. Give descriptive feedback.**

- Reteach or regroup for those needing more practice.
- Extend or elaborate for more able learners.

- Notice who has difficulty and for whom this is easy.
- Provide more support for individuals and groups, as well as extensions for the more able students.

Implications for the Classroom

Brain research confirms what we know from education research: that educators must make provisions for individual differences in learning styles by providing alternative grouping arrangements, instructional materials, time frames, and so on.

(Paradis, Nicoladis, and Genesee, 2000)

All students benefit from varied instructional tactics and activities that enhance what we know about learning (Sousa, 2007), engage the multiple intelligences, and accommodate diverse learning styles (McCarthy, 1981).

By using a variety of instructional tactics (Bennett and Rolheiser, 2001), teachers are able to differentiate the learning of diverse students and groups in appropriate ways. Here are examples of some tactics that FSL teachers may use to incorporate and use assessment information and to differentiate teaching and learning.

Before a New Text is Explored...

Appendix A
See Anticipation Guide.

Appendix A
See Word Wall/ Vocabulary Bank.

Appendix A
See Learning Log/ Journal.

Appendix A
See Draw What I Say.

Teachers...	Students...
• monitor students' ability to access prior knowledge and experience, in order to activate connections to the topic and set purposes for learning something new in French.	• complete an Anticipation Guide or answer anticipation questions orally.
• assess needs for further vocabulary and structures before launching into the content to gauge student readiness.	• recall previously-learned vocabulary. • participate in building a Word Wall or Vocabulary Bank. • scan the text looking for and identifying cognates and familiar words.
• set a purpose for exploring text and develop criteria and models for successful student participation. • share the purpose of the learning sequence, the product, and expectations with students and parents.	• contribute to designing the project and the learning sequence. • discover the steps to succeed in the learning task (on chart paper or on a rubric). • complete the first step of a Learning Log. • discuss what they are learning at home.
• provide differing expectations for the more able and less able student so that all students reach their potential.	• complete personalized tasks when appropriate.
• plan to incorporate a variety of musical, rhythmical, manipulative, and kinesthetic activities into various learning stages and projects to engage the multiple intelligences.	• engage in a variety of active learning tasks which combine language, drama, art, movement, such as Draw What I Say and Total Physical Response.

During the Exploration of a Text...

Teachers...	Students...
• structure groupings and partners to support student needs.	• feel secure trying new language with a partner or in a group.
• provide audio and visual support for texts to allow for more than one learning style and preferred mode (visual, auditory).	• listen to the text being read, then read independently.
• use rhyme, rhythm, and repetition in meaningful ways when practising vocabulary to assist memory with mnemonics and multiple intelligences.	• find learning fun and repetition and practice more engaging.
• help students code the text in concrete ways—using sticky notes or highlighters, etc.—in order to build connections and comprehension.	• focus on the text rather than the meaning of each individual word, and make connections. – J'identifie des mots familiers. – J'identifie des mots-amis. – Je fais des liens. – Je suis d'accord. / Je ne suis pas d'accord.
• provide graphic organizers to aid students' meaning-making.	• record key ideas in manageable pieces.
• use focused questioning techniques such as Numbered Heads to tailor questions and make students accountable.	• are ready to answer and will experience success.
• use strategies for rehearsal, repetition, and involvement to provide a structure for guided practice and language use.	• practise language in a low risk context. • are held accountable for listening to their partner in an AB Partnering situation.
• circulate to assess individual progress, conference with individual students, and provide further support as necessary using Assessment *for* Learning Tools.	• know that the teacher will help them be successful. The more able students are further challenged.
• use a Traffic Light to gauge students' understanding of language, instructions, or tasks.	• learn to be aware of their learning.
• provide self-assessment opportunities based on clear expectations to involve students in thinking about their learning.	• have an ongoing Learning Log or portfolio to demonstrate and track their learning. • complete portions of a shared assessment after each step. • have opportunities to share authentic learning with parents.

Appendix A
See Coding a Text.

Appendix A
See Venn Diagram, and Fish Bone.

Appendix A
See Numbered Heads.

Appendix A
See AB Partnering.

Appendix A
See Assessment for Learning Tools.

Appendix A
See Traffic Light.

Appendix A
See Learning Log/Journal

After Exploring the Text...

Teachers...	Students...
• provide choice for projects and tasks to engage all students and give as many opportunities for success as possible.	• incorporate their personalities, strengths, and interests into the use of French. • use information and communication technology to share their learning with an authentic audience (e.g., KidPix®, PowerPoint®).
• look at assessment rubrics co-constructed with students at the outset of the task to reflect on what was accomplished.	• organize production pieces in a Portfolio, and reflect on learning achieved in a Learning Log.
• provide Sentence Starters and Models, and Anchor Charts to help students reflect and set future goals.	• set new goals based on self-assessment. • express their reflections in a supported manner.

Appendix A
See Portfolio and Learning Log/Journal.

Appendix A
See Anchor Chart, and Sentence Starters and Models.

In Summary...

- Assessing and differentiating are tightly interwoven at every step throughout the teaching and learning process.

- Teachers plan for differentiation before they begin a learning sequence and react to students' needs during the learning sequence by re-teaching or providing an alternative approach.

- Teachers and students engage in shared assessment in order to understand FSL learning processes and set further goals.

Professional Learning Survey

A. Consider using a learning log to explore and track your professional learning at several points in time—before or after reading this module, or while trying out an idea.

1. What do I do in the planning phase to address the diverse learning needs of my students? To what degree does this differentiation succeed in meeting their needs?

2. How do I adjust individual and small group instruction for the more able and less able learners? To what degree are these adjustments successful?

3. What types of adjustments do I make during a lesson to address the diverse learning needs of my students? To what degree does this differentiation succeed in meeting the needs of all my students?

4. How and when do I assess my students' learning? To what degree do I use these assessments to make adjustments to my teaching?

5. How do I involve students in assessing and improving their own learning? What types of assessment do I use?

B. What are your professional learning goals at this time?

1. I would like to advance my knowledge and understanding of…

2. I would like to try the following ideas from this module with the goal to…

C. Indicate your professional growth at this time by shading the following continuum, where 1 represents the beginning of your experimentation and 5 represents significant progress.

1. I adjust my teaching before and during instruction, to address the diverse learning needs of my students, and after instruction in response to student assessment and success.

Date		1	2	3	4	5

Activating Strategies: Making Connections

BIG IDEA 5

- Students use literacy strategies in their first language to reinforce and enhance learning in a second language; literacy strategies learned in a second language reinforce learning in the first language.

- Learning is enhanced when students make connections to their own experiences, interests, knowledge, and cultural identity through exploration of rich, meaningful texts.

Introduction

> It is important to activate students' prior knowledge because students may not explicitly realize what they know about a particular topic or issue; consequently, their prior knowledge may not facilitate learning unless it is brought to consciousness.
>
> *(Cummins, 1995)*

As FSL teachers, we may be challenged by the prospect of using text in the FSL classroom. By importing the strategies and tactics used in other subject areas, we will not only be able to facilitate the transfer of skills, but also provide support for students as they explore texts and undertake tasks that are cognitively challenging, yet linguistically appropriate. Students bring many skills to FSL from their backgrounds as content learners and, in some cases, as additional language learners. Here, we focus on pre-existing skills that we believe are most effective in moving students along the continuum of language and literacy learning in FSL. Though they have been mentioned throughout the previous four sections, we will now consider how teachers can facilitate their transfer and use in the FSL context.

Tapping into Students' Pre-existing Literacy Skills

Most second-language learners possess substantial conceptual knowledge and well-developed communication skills in their first language. They have used text for a number of years to learn, seek enjoyment and, increasingly, to explore and communicate ideas and information via technological means. The different types of text that students encounter in the FSL class should be as varied, appealing, and connected to their interests and needs as the texts are in their first language.

Instruction in the FSL classroom begins with what students already know and build on that foundation. Many of the same teaching and learning strategies used in other areas of students' lives may be used to develop literacy in

French; however, teachers and students will likely need to adapt them depending on experience with the strategies, amount of scaffolding, difficulty of text, learner attributes, and so on. It is perhaps useful to consider literacy learning on a continuum of skills and strategies that range from those used in the first language to those used in the second language. FSL teachers can work in concert with teachers in other subject areas to help move students along the literacy continuum.

A Literacy Learning Continuum

First-language skills and Strategies → First-language skills and strategies transferable to second-language learning → Second-language skills and strategies

> The L2 [second-language] learner juggles language and literacy because he/she inhabits two zones of proximal development.
>
> *(Daniel, 2005)*

In the FSL class, students develop their language competence while using cognitively stimulating material that is age- and grade-appropriate in formats that respect their linguistic level in the second or additional language. The difference between these two levels can be very frustrating for second-language students because their level of ease and skill is greatly reduced in French.

Learning theory indicates that we learn best when pushed just beyond our comfort zone of knowledge and skills into the Zone of Proximal Development (Vygotsky, 1962, 1978). This zone is the instructional level at which careful modelling, group work, problem solving, and teacher input are very important. Students generally experience a lower threshold of challenge in the second language than in the first language, so teachers must balance these different cognitive and linguistic developmental levels by careful sequencing of activities and using scaffolding to provide challenge without frustration.

[handwritten margin notes: anxiety not linking; constructive frustration (disequilibrium); vs opt-out]

> For more on the Zone of Proximal Development, see Big Idea 1, p. 29.

The FSL teacher can scaffold learning in a number of ways:

- Linking new information to personal experience and prior knowledge, both in terms of content and language; for example, building on an environmental theme that is also being taught in Science and about which students have some knowledge and opinions.

- Highlighting familiar content and format features in the text; reassuring students that they can already recognize key information in a text before even tackling the language or content.

- Linking the written word to oral language; showing students that they have already used some of the language they are now seeing in the text.

- Pointing out how strategies and tactics used in the FSL classroom can be used in other subject areas, and vice versa, for example, by adapting familiar tactics, such as thinking aloud, using cooperative group practices, and representing understanding on graphic organizers.

> Nowhere is the role of prior knowledge more important than in second-language learning contexts. Students who can access their prior knowledge through the language and culture most familiar to them can call on a rich array of schemata, whereas students who believe they can only use the knowledge they have learned in the second language are limited in their access.
>
> *(Chamot, 1998)*

Validating Students' Cultural and Linguistic Backgrounds and Identities

For students whose first language is neither English nor French, there are extra connections possible, since these students possess linguistic and cultural backgrounds and skills that can serve them well in learning French as an additional language. For example, teachers can help enhance these connections by becoming informed about students' languages. Where many languages are represented in a class, students can be encouraged to teach their teacher and peers about their language so that connections can become apparent. As much as possible, texts must acknowledge and validate the experiences of students, whatever their backgrounds. Beyond the inclusion of cultural festivals, texts should reflect the potential diversity of life experiences. Where it may be difficult to have one text meet all of the optimal criteria, students can be encouraged to create text that reflects their experiences.

> "Prior knowledge refers not only to knowledge or skills previously acquired in [formal instruction] but also to [the totality of the] experiences that have shaped the learner's identity and cognitive functioning. In classrooms with students from linguistically diverse backgrounds, instruction should explicitly activate this knowledge.
>
> *(Cummins, 2001)*

As well, there are common underlying skills used in many school subjects, such as sequencing, generalizing, and problem solving. These cognitive processes, as we know, are not compartmentalized into the discrete curriculum areas and can be developed in a non subject-specific way. Therefore, even though the content may differ, the foundational similarities prevail. In the same way, although differences between two languages are distinct, there are underlying cognitive processes that are very similar. The hypothesis put forth in this theory, called the Dual-iceberg Theory (Cummins, 1984), is that first-language proficiencies can be transferred to second-language learning, and vice versa.

Figure 8

The Dual-iceberg Representation of Bilingual Proficiency

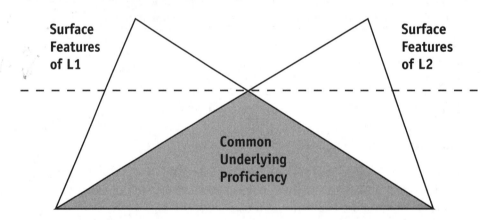

Adapted from: Cummins, J. *Bilingualism and Special Education: Issues in Assessment and Pedagogy.* San Diego, CA: College Hill Press, 1984.

> "Intellectual development... is not compartmentalized according to topics of instruction.
>
> *(Vygotsky, 1962)*

French can provide a foundational experience, particularly for students who have gaps in their prior education, and thus less of an iceberg base. For example, whereas other subjects may have complex cognitive concepts to be understood in the students' second language (English), French offers a subject where success is not dependent on prior English knowledge. French is a subject where English language learners may actually feel more on par with their peers than in other subjects.

Appendix A
See Plus-Minus-Interesting Chart.

Learning a new language gives some learners a second chance to acquire important literacy skills in their first language. Focusing on key information by deselecting details is a skill that may become clear to a student working with a French text in ways that may not have been mastered in English Language Arts or Social Studies. A reciprocal reinforcement of skills and strategies becomes possible when, for example, a Plus-Minus-Interesting Chart is used to record information about how to care for animals when exploring a French text and is also being used as a tactic in Science.

Using Language in Meaningful Ways

In the past, learning a second language in school often meant learning it out of context—studying it rather than using it in a meaningful way. Students became very good at *knowing* French but not speaking or understanding it in real-world situations.

FSL students need to be exposed to language in many forms, and they need to understand and use it in order to learn. According to Krashen's input hypothesis (1982), a student's acquisition of a second language progresses by receiving input that is one step beyond his or her level of linguistic competence. In other words, the student is exposed to text in which he or she understands most, but not all, parts. The other important part of the language learning equation is output, or language produced by the student. Students need many opportunities to communicate, use, and reuse language to perform tasks and for the teacher to model, interact, and monitor what they produce (Swain, 1985).

EXAMPLE

In a learning sequence on pastimes, the teacher may introduce expressions, such as *J'aime nager* or *J'aime jouer du piano*, once students have already learned how to express preferences by using *J'aime…* or *Je préfère…* (e.g, *les fruits, du chocolat*) in previous learning sequences.

Second-language theory supports teachers as language models, texts as sources of content, and real communication as the best ways to advance second-language learning. Teachers help students understand input by selecting texts that are appropriate to their students' proficiency and interests. They support meaning with visuals, examples, gestures, repetition, and strategic tools. Students then need to use language in order to learn it and to understand the connection between oral and written language. They also need to experience language in real contexts that engage their cognitive level but are accessible to their linguistic level. This balance is not easy to achieve and requires support in terms of having the right texts and sufficient scaffolding.

The best conditions for meaningful FSL learning are when students work with text that is as authentic and as varied as possible with opportunities to demonstrate their learning in personally significant ways.

Overview

Using Rich and Varied Text

> Learning strategies are specific actions taken by the learner to make learning easier, faster, more enjoyable, more self-directed, more effective, and more transferable to new situations.
>
> *(Oxford, 1990)*

Making meaning from text is a complex activity. Students need to make sense of what they see and hear by understanding messages, connecting them to what they already know, and finding ways to work through the unknown. Even though students may not understand all parts of a given text, it is important to present content in a realistic, context-rich format.

Good learners check their understanding as they explore text. When they encounter problems, they choose appropriate strategies to clarify their understanding. It is important, therefore, that students acquire transferable strategies that will help them to access, manage, organize, and assess information in an increasing range of situations. The purpose of teaching and using learning strategies is to help students think and learn.

Learning Strategies in a Literacy Context

Learning strategies are specific actions or techniques students use to enhance their own learning (Scarcella and Oxford, 1992). In the early stages of developing literacy strategies and skills in FSL, the teacher's role is to encourage students to reproduce and organize what they learn from various texts. With experience and increasing linguistic and strategic competence, teachers and students move along the literacy continuum to more independent and creative interactions with text.

Developing Learning Strategies and Skills in FSL

A Literacy Learning Continuum

- list
- point out
- quote
- repeat

- classify
- give examples
- group
- identify
- predict
- select

- combine
- compare
- organize
- reconstruct
- substitute
- summarize

- dramatize
- simulate

- analyze
- critique

- adapt
- augment
- create

The scaffolding, guiding, and coaching of learning strategies by teachers is critical to student success in FSL learning. Strategies are modelled first by the teacher, then practised by students as they engage with and understand texts. Some strategies are cognitive in nature—concerned with how students learn. Others are metacognitive—concerned with thinking about one's learning. Here are a few examples of what these look like in an FSL classroom:

Cognitive	Rehearsing: repeating the names of items;
	Organizing: grouping and classifying words and ideas;
	Inferencing: guessing meanings of new items and predicting outcomes;
	Summarizing: synthesizing what has been heard or read.
Metacognitive	Planning: organizing a written or spoken task;
	Monitoring: reviewing one's attention to a task;
	Evaluating: checking comprehension or presentation of learning after a task.

Implications for the Classroom

Strategic Tools in Language Learning

Many of the tactics and graphic organizers that can serve as strategic tools in FSL are identical to those students already using in English. They can be helpful in showing students that they know more in French than they might think. The more connections teachers make between *what* and *how* students are learning in FSL with *what* and *how* they are learning in other subject areas, the more useful these strategic tools become.

Venn Diagrams, used to identify similarities and differences between elements of a text, are familiar to many students. Consider the use of the following Venn in a Social Studies class:

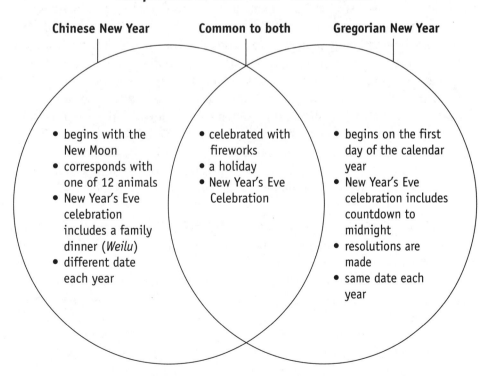

Comparison of New Years' Celebrations

Chinese New Year   **Common to both**   **Gregorian New Year**

- begins with the New Moon
- corresponds with one of 12 animals
- New Year's Eve celebration includes a family dinner (*Weilu*)
- different date each year

- celebrated with fireworks
- a holiday
- New Year's Eve Celebration

- begins on the first day of the calendar year
- New Year's Eve celebration includes countdown to midnight
- resolutions are made
- same date each year

To conduct a similar activity in the FSL class, the teacher might choose to simplify the range of language as in the following example. Students may use a combination of words and phrases heard or viewed in the text, symbols and/or illustrations to represent their ideas.

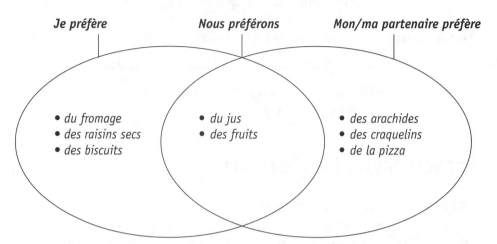

Je compare les collations préférées dans la classe

| Je préfère | Nous préférons | Mon/ma partenaire préfère |

- du fromage
- des raisins secs
- des biscuits

- du jus
- des fruits

- des arachides
- des craquelins
- de la pizza

Appendix A
See Anticipation Guide, Inquiry Chart, K-W-L and K-W-L Plus Charts, Story Map, and Place Mat.

The use of strategic tools helps to organize students' thinking. However, some of the tools that students use in other subjects, such as concept mapping, character analysis, and so on, are less applicable in elementary FSL where students do not yet have a broad language base. Others can be simplified for use in FSL, such as Anticipation Guides (Herber, 1978), Inquiry Charts (Hoffman, 1992), K-W-L and K-W-L Plus Charts (Carr and Ogle, 1987), Story Maps (Beck and McKeown, 1981), and Place Mat (Bennett, Rolheiser, and Stevahn, 1991).

Appendix A
See Anchor Chart, Sentence Starters and Models, and Word Wall/ Vocabulary Bank.

Teachers can assist students in making meaning from text by emphasizing familiar French words and cognates, pointing out visual and context clues to help with understanding of new words, and encouraging predictions. They can tailor their questioning by starting with *oui / non* questions or giving two alternate answers and having students choose and repeat one of them. They can also use gesture and mime, draw attention to textual cues and visuals, and refer to Anchor Charts. Students may convey understanding by using copied texts, Sentence Starters and Models, Word Wall/Vocabulary Banks, symbols, illustrations, and other tools and formats. Again, teachers need to think of the continuum of what is possible in the beginning and what becomes possible with experience with the language and the tools.

> Metacognition refers to a learner's awareness of task objectives, the ability to use and evaluate learning strategies, and the capacity to monitor progress and adjust learning behaviors to accommodate their learning needs.
>
> *(Flavell, 1979)*

Strategies to Help Students Develop Metacognitive Skills

In language learning, students can become aware of and manage their own learning. Research shows that effective text users think about *how* they think. Some of the ways FSL teachers can help students make connections while they are learning is by tapping into known strategies, making them evident, and then teaching new ones. It is not enough to demonstrate how to explore text; teachers must explain as they model (thinking aloud) in order to focus students on what they should be doing as text users. The objective is that students will eventually use these strategies on their own.

In listening contexts...	In reading and viewing contexts...	In oral interaction contexts...
• *Je cherche des mots familiers.* • *J'utilise le contexte.* • *Je fais des prédictions.* • *Je fais des liens.*	• *Je lis les titres.* • *Je regarde les images.* • *Je regarde le format.* • *J'identifie des mots familiers.* • *Je fais des liens.* • *Je trouve les idées importantes.*	• *Je pose des questions.* • *Je fais des prédictions.* • *Je fais des efforts pour parler français.* • *Je communique mes idées.*

Teachers model and coach the use of this language as they demonstrate how to apply each learning strategy. They may use tools, such as Anchor Charts, to provide support.

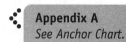

Appendix A
See Anchor Chart.

Before a New Text is Explored...

Teachers...	Students...
• ask general questions to help students make personal connections to the text.	• focus on visuals in texts.
• teach students to recognize patterns in language and show how these can help them make meaning.	• make predictions, initially using images and words, then words and sentences.
• provide different formats (for example, audio, visual, film, and textual) of the same content to reinforce learning.	• make connections to other subject areas and prior content knowledge.
• model learning strategies so that students see and begin to use them.	• form mental pictures of the text to be heard, viewed, or read, for example, by drawing them.

During the Exploration of a Text...

Teachers...	Students...
• incorporate facial expressions, gestures, and other techniques to assist with meaning-making.	• use three of the five senses to make meaning.
• read and re-read text aloud with students, pausing to check understanding (point out the visuals, captions, labels, special features).	• pay attention to text features. • focus on what is most important in the text and how the ideas fit together.
• invite students to repeat aloud key ideas or chant recurring words or phrases.	• highlight key words or ideas. • mark sections where additional information is needed.
• restate some of the text's main ideas in other words or with supporting visuals.	• sketch or make notes. • re-read the text.
• provide graphic organizers, such as charts, webs, and Timelines to assist meaning-making.	• transfer key information from the text onto a graphic organizer.

After Exploring the Text...

Teachers...	Students...
• retell the story or ideas in a variety of ways, for example, by referring to the images.	• sequence the text—using the text itself and/or images related to the text. • identify questions that have been answered by the text, initially using question stems.
• provide graphic organizers to represent understanding, initially with model answers or information gaps.	• use a graphic organizer to represent what has been learned in the text, initially recording key ideas or facts and figures.
• ensure that students use and reuse oral language before producing written language.	• share opinions about the text with other text users, for example, in the class or on-line with others (a book rap by e-mail).
• provide varied opportunities to respond, e.g., aural, visual, or written products using different media.	• transform the information into a new form, for example, a poster, role play, brochure, PowerPoint® presentation, cheer. • work with others to organize, share, and/or present what has been learned.
• take time to debrief and reflect on learning strategies.	• record reflections on learning, initially as checklists, symbols, and illustrations moving to use of sentence stems, then to other forms of expression.

In Summary...

- Literacy strategies are transferable from first-language to second-language learning, and vice versa.

- Pointing out the connections between first- and second-language learning helps students realize that they can link their learning in FSL to learning in general.

- Meaningful learning occurs when students work with text that is authentic and varied, with opportunities to demonstrate learning in personally significant ways.

- Rather than focusing on one strategy to understand *one text*, students develop a repertoire of strategies to use for *all texts*.

- If we consider these learning strategies on a literacy continuum, students can move to higher levels of skill or complexity as they gain experience and success with the various strategies.

Professional Learning Survey

A. Consider using a learning log to explore and track your professional learning at several points in time—before or after reading this module, or while trying out an idea.

   1. What types of texts do I choose for my students? To what degree are these texts accessible but also rich enough to capture and hold their interest?

   2. What types of projects or tasks do I choose for my students? How do I validate the varied backgrounds of my students?

   3. What types of strategic tools (instructional tactics and graphic organizers) do I incorporate to help students organize their thinking around a particular text? Which ones are they already familiar with in their English curriculum?

   4. How do I scaffold learning for my students, that is, break up their learning into manageable steps? What are some teaching and learning strategies I use *before*, *during*, and *after* exploring the text?

   5. To what degree do I move my students along the literacy learning continuum, for example, moving from listening and repeating language from a text to grouping and comparing ideas and information?

B. What are your professional learning goals at this time?

   1. I would like to advance my knowledge and understanding of…

   2. I would like to try the following ideas from this module with the goal to…

C. Indicate your professional growth at this time by shading the following continuum, where 1 represents the beginning of your experimentation and 5 represents significant progress.

   1. I use a variety of teaching and learning strategies to help my students *learn how to learn* in FSL.

Date	1	2	3	4	5

Comprehension Strategies for Listening, Viewing, and Reading

Gradual Release of Responsibility Legend:

 Think Aloud: Teacher modelling

Shared Practice: Teacher modelling with student participation

Guided and Independent Practice: Student practice with teacher guidance

Exploring aural, visual, and written text in FSL should be about understanding the text. It should also be about acquiring new strategies, or reusing strategies that students have already acquired from first language instruction, to help them maximize understanding. Effective text users call on a number of strategies as they engage in text that leads to understanding. Bringing these strategies to a conscious level, so that students are aware of how the strategies help them understand text, is called metacognition or thinking about how we think. Applying strategies helps students become independent text users.

In the following pages, we will focus on strategies that teachers may use with students to facilitate comprehension of text within an FSL context. Specific strategies are used *before, during*, or *after* exploring a text. They are best introduced in short lessons that require very simple but meaningful input from students. They should also be introduced in a progressive manner so that one strategy becomes familiar and comfortable for students before another is introduced. Anchor charts help cue and reinforce the language used to talk about each strategy. These charts may easily be referred to in subsequent lessons.

The strategies that follow are numbered for easy reference, but they need not be used in this order. A particular strategy may lend itself better to one text than another.

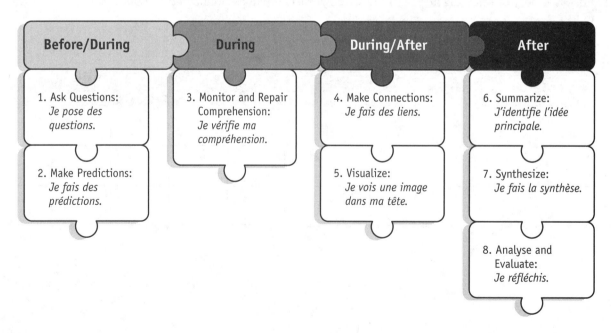

Before/During	During	During/After	After
1. Ask Questions: *Je pose des questions.*	3. Monitor and Repair Comprehension: *Je vérifie ma compréhension.*	4. Make Connections: *Je fais des liens.*	6. Summarize: *J'identifie l'idée principale.*
2. Make Predictions: *Je fais des prédictions.*		5. Visualize: *Je vois une image dans ma tête.*	7. Synthesize: *Je fais la synthèse.*
			8. Analyse and Evaluate: *Je réfléchis.*

How to Use the Comprehension Strategies

Teachers follow specific steps as they develop comprehension strategies with students to help them listen to, view, and read various types of texts. Eight comprehension strategies used by effective text users are presented in this section. The steps explicitly teaching each strategy are organized in the following way:

Steps for Explicit Teaching of Strategies in FSL	Description	En français, on dit...
Introduce the Strategy	The teacher introduces a strategy and provides students with simple language cues to actively use the strategy.	– *Voici une stratégie.*
Model the Strategy	The teacher uses a Think Aloud to articulate how they are using the strategy. They use facial expressions, gestures, and non-verbal cues to support comprehension. With the help of these forms of articulation, students are able to visualize the otherwise invisible in-the-head strategies that proficient learners use to support comprehension.	– *Moi, je le fais; vous, vous observez.*
Practise the Strategy	**Shared Practice** Several students are invited to work with the teacher. They use the strategies with the teacher in order to adapt the model provided to reflect their personal situation.	– *Moi, je le fais; vous, vous m'aidez.*
	Guided Practice Students work in pairs or small groups. They use the strategies with their peers as teachers support and coach them.	– *Toi et ton ami(e), vous le faites; moi, je vous aide.*
	Independent Practice Students work independently. As students become more skilled in using new strategies through guided practice, the teacher allows students to work more independently.	– *Vous, vous le faites; moi, j'observe.*
Reflect on the Strategy	Students reflect on how using the strategy helps them understand the text. Teachers guide students' reflection using a variety of approaches.	– *Qu'est-ce que vous faites pour comprendre le texte?*

By following these steps, teachers gradually release responsibility for using the strategies to students. Teachers provide independent practice opportunities for students to use the strategies and processes alone or with peers, asking for help as needed. Teachers monitor students' ability to use the strategy and revisit steps depending on students' needs.

1. Ask Questions: *Je pose des questions.*

Questions that help second-language learners identify the context and activate their prior knowledge and experiences with the topic will help them understand new aural, visual, and written texts. Teachers model this strategy by asking appropriate questions that verify student comprehension, activate prior knowledge, and develop students' language use. Appropriate questions would include those that require more than a *oui / non* answer and those that invite students to talk about their own experiences with the topic. Having students ask themselves questions helps them approach a text in a more successful way.

Introduce the Strategy

To aid comprehension, students benefit from a simple explanation of the strategy that they are going to use. This can be done by displaying a visual or several visuals for the strategy, illustrating the key language cues that students may use to talk about the strategy. These cues may be displayed on strategy cards, anchor charts, or on acetates for an overhead projector.

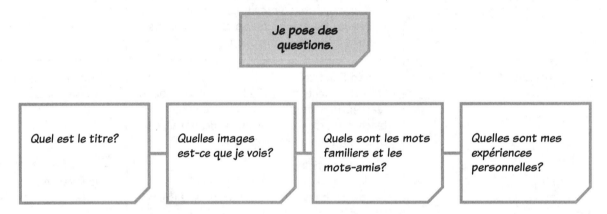

Je pose des questions.

| Quel est le titre? | Quelles images est-ce que je vois? | Quels sont les mots familiers et les mots-amis? | Quelles sont mes expériences personnelles? |

Since learning to use a strategy is an ongoing process, frequent references to the strategy using different texts will help students internalize its use. Consider introducing one language cue at a time to make strategy lessons short and simple. In this way, students will develop a repertoire of language cues and strategies over the course of the school year.

Model the Strategy

Whether the text is aural, visual, or written, it is helpful for students to look at an image on an overhead or in large format to focus their attention. If the text is aural, the image may be on a worksheet or a visual supplied by the teacher; if it is a visual text, it may be an image taken from the video; or if it is written, it may be the cover of the book. Model the "Ask Questions" strategy in a Think Aloud.

Teachers think aloud while modelling the strategy, stopping at strategic points to demonstrate important literacy skills while monitoring student comprehension. Teachers ask and answer the questions as they model so students understand how to use the strategy.

See model language for Think Aloud, Shared and Guided Practice, and Reflection, p. 76.

Practise the Strategy

Students look at the visuals and the title of the text and ask questions to practise the strategy. A graphic organizer is one method of recording students' answers as they ask questions. In the four sections of the organizer, they record and/or illustrate the answers to the questions. Teachers help students practise the strategy. When students are ready, they will apply the strategy to the remaining text.

See Fiche d'activité 1 : Je pose des questions, p. 77.

To simplify:	To add challenge:

• Offer students a choice of responses to help them with new vocabulary.
  – *Est-ce que vous voyez un garçon ou une fille?*
	• Ask questions to draw out the content of an image.
	  – *Qui? Quoi? Quand? Comment? Où? Pourquoi?*

Reflect on the Strategy

In a teacher-led class discussion, students share the answers to the questions they asked themselves to help them understand the text. Teachers guide students, using their answers on the graphic organizer, as they explain how their questions aided their understanding.

Assessment for Learning

Do students...
- look at the visuals to help themselves identify the topic and/or the context?
- look at visuals to help themselves understand?
- identify prior knowledge related to the topic?
- make connections to their prior experience with the topic?
- identify words that they recognize (e.g., *mots familiers, mots-amis*)?
- record appropriate information about the questions?

Model Language
Ask Questions: *Je pose des questions.*

In the following examples, students plan a menu for a social event. Teachers use a Think Aloud as students listen to, view, or read a text on snacks.

Modelling
Moi, je le fais; vous, vous observez.

Think Aloud: Aural, Visual, and Written Text
- *Je pose des questions.*
- *Quel est le titre?* Ah! C'est «Mes collations préférées».
- *Quelles images est-ce que je vois?* Ah! Je vois un garçon. Je vois des tacos.
- *J'écoute / je regarde / je lis une partie du texte. Quels sont les mots familiers et les mots-amis?* Hmm… «Un taco» est un mot-ami. «J'aime» est un mot familier.
- *Quelles sont mes expériences personnelles?* Hmm… Moi, je préfère les burritos.

Shared Practice
Moi, je le fais; vous, vous m'aidez.

Shared Practice: Aural, Visual, and Written Text
- *Je pose des questions.*
- *Quel est le titre? (C'est _____.)*
- *Quelles images est-ce que je vois? (Je vois _____. Je vois _____.)*
- *Quels sont les mots familiers et les mots-amis? (_____ est un mot familier. _____ est un mot-ami.)*
- *Quelles sont mes expériences personnelles? (Moi, j'aime / je n'aime pas _____.)*

Guided Practice: Aural, Visual, and Written Text
- *Quelle question est-ce que vous posez en premier? (Quel est le titre?)*
- *Excellent! Qui peut répondre à la question? (C'est _____.)*
- *Quelle question est-ce que vous posez ensuite? (Quelles images est-ce que je vois?)*
- *Et qui peut répondre à la question? (Je vois _____.)*
- *Parfait! Et quelle question est-ce que vous posez maintenant? (Quels sont les mots familiers et les mots-amis?)*
- *Et qui peut répondre à la question? (_____ est un mot familier. _____ est un mot-ami.)*
- *Très bien. Et quelle question est-ce que vous posez enfin? (Quelles sont mes expériences personnelles?)*
- *Et qui peut répondre à la question? (Je _____.)*

Guided Practice
Toi et ton ami(e) vous le faites; moi, je vous aide.

Independent Practice
Vous, vous le faites; moi, j'observe.

Reflection: Aural, Visual, and Written Text
- *Qu'est-ce que je fais pour comprendre? Est-ce que j'utilise le titre? les images? les mots familiers et les mots-amis? mes expériences personnelles?*
- *Quelle(s) question(s) est-ce que je pose?*

Nom : _____ Date : _____ **Fiche d'activité 1**

Je pose des questions. _____

Je réponds aux questions.

Quel est le titre? **Qu'est-ce que c'est?** _____	**Quelles images est-ce que je vois?** _____ _____
Je pose des questions.	
Quels sont les mots familiers et les mots-amis? _____ _____ _____	**Quelles sont mes expériences personnelles?** _____ _____

2. Make Predictions: *Je fais des prédictions.*

After students have used questioning strategies to identify the context and personalize the topic by linking it to their prior experiences, they can begin to make predictions about the meaning of the text. These predictions will be based on their exploration of the title, visuals, and familiar vocabulary. Making predictions helps students approach a text in a more purposeful way. When students anticipate the subject of a text, they are able to comprehend the text more easily.

Introduce the Strategy

To aid comprehension, students benefit from a simple explanation of the strategy that they are going to use. This can be done by displaying a visual or several visuals for the strategy, illustrating the key language cues that students may use to talk about the strategy. These cues may be displayed on strategy cards, anchor charts, or on acetates for an overhead projector.

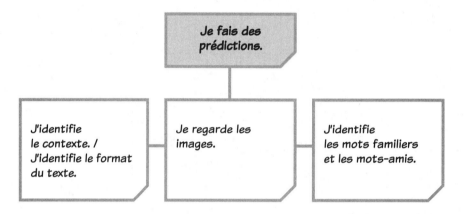

Since learning to use a strategy is an ongoing process, frequent references to the strategy using different texts will help students internalize its use. Consider introducing one language cue at a time to make strategy lessons short and simple. In this way, students will develop a repertoire of language cues and strategies over the course of the school year.

Model the Strategy

Teachers may use the text to have students anticipate the content of the text and make predictions. If it is an aural text, they may listen to a part of the selection and identify the context and familiar words or cognates. If it is a visual or written text, students may look at the cues (text format, visuals, title, familiar words, and cognates) on overhead or in large format. In both cases, students observe the prediction process while the teacher models it using a think aloud.

See model language for Think Aloud, Shared and Guided Practice, and Reflection, pp. 80–81.

Practise the Strategy

Teachers help students as they practise the strategy. They examine the title, the visuals, and text format or context, and then listen or look for familiar words. Based on the clues they identify, they make predictions about the text. Students use the strategy of making and verifying predictions as they explore the text, first with the teacher and, later, independently.

See Fiche d'activité 2 : Je fais des prédictions, pp. 82–83.

To simplify:	To add challenge:

• Provide students with specific choices to help them successfully make predictions. Simple *est-ce que* questions can be used.
  – *Est-ce que c'est une chanson ou une description? (C'est une _____.)*
	• Ask students to explain the clues they used to make their predictions.
	  – *Pourquoi est-ce que vous pensez que c'est le magasin «Sports illimités»?*
	  – *Quels sont les indices?*

Reflect on the Strategy

Once the students have finished making their predictions about the text, they are ready to share them with their classmates. They can also share the clues and knowledge they used to make these predictions, so that their peers can follow their reasoning and perhaps comment on their appropriateness. After they have finished working with the text, they revisit their predictions and compare them to the actual results of the text. This will provide students with the opportunity to self-assess the effectiveness of the strategies they used to make the predictions.

Assessment for Learning

Do students...

- look at the visuals to find clues to make predictions?

- identify prior knowledge related to the topic to make predictions?

- identify familiar words (e.g., *mots-amis, mots familiers*) to make predictions?

- record appropriate information about their predictions?

- verify if their predictions are correct?

Model Language
Make Predictions: *Je fais des prédictions.*

In the following examples, students are preparing to shop with an adult for new clothes in anticipation of the new school season. They may listen to, view, or read a text describing clothes that are available at several stores. Students then predict which advertisement corresponds to each store.

Modelling
Moi, je le fais; vous, vous observez.

Think Aloud: Aural, Visual, and Written Text

- *J'écoute / je regarde / je lis le texte.*

- *J'identifie le contexte. Qu'est-ce que c'est?*

- *Hmm... C'est une publicité pour des vêtements.* (for aural text)

- *J'identifie le format du texte.*

- *C'est une publicité pour des vêtements.* (for visual and written text)

- *Je regarde les images.*

- *Je vois un t-shirt et un pantalon.*

- *J'identifie les mots familiers et les mots-amis.*

- *Hmm... «Sportif» est un mot familier et «un t-shirt» est un mot-ami.*

- *Je fais des prédictions.*

- *Je pense que c'est le magasin «Sports illimités».*

- *J'écoute / je regarde / je lis le texte une deuxième fois. Je vérifie ma prédiction.*

Shared Practice
Moi, je le fais; et vous, vous m'aidez.

Shared Practice: Aural, Visual, and Written Text

- *J'écoute / je regarde / je lis le texte.*

- *J'identifie le contexte. (C'est _____.)* (for aural text)

- *J'identifie le format du texte. (C'est _____.)* (for visual and written text)

- *Je regarde les images. (Je vois _____. Je vois _____.)*

- *J'identifie les mots familiers et les mots-amis. (_____ est un mot familier. _____ est un mot-ami.)*

- *Je fais des prédictions. (Je pense que c'est _____.)*

- *J'écoute / je regarde / je lis le texte une deuxième fois. Je vérifie ma prédiction.*

Guided Practice: Aural, Visual, and Written Text

- *Qu'est-ce que vous faites en premier? (J'identifie le contexte.) (for aural text)*

- *Qu'est-ce que vous faites en premier? (J'identifie le format du texte.) (for visual and written text)*

- *Très bien! Qu'est-ce que c'est? (C'est _____.)*

- *Et ensuite? (Je regarde les images.)*

- *C'est ça. Qu'est-ce que vous voyez? (Je vois _____ et je vois _____.)*

- *Et ensuite? (J'identifie les mots familiers et les mots-amis.)*

- *Super! Quels sont les mots familiers et les mots-amis? (_____ est un mot familier et _____ est un mot-ami.)*

- *Bon. Alors, quelles sont vos prédictions? (Je pense que c'est _____.)*

- *Parfait! Qu'est-ce que vous faites maintenant? (Je relis. Je vérifie ma prédiction.)*

Guided Practice
Toi et ton ami(e), vous le faites; moi, je vous aide.

Independent Practice
Vous, vous le faites; moi, j'observe.

Reflection: Aural, Visual, and Written Text

- *Regardez vos prédictions.*
- *Est-ce que vos prédictions sont justes?*

Écoutons! Regardons!

Je fais des prédictions.

Avant d'écouter le texte, je fais des prédictions.

Le texte :

_____

1. J'identifie le contexte.
C'est

_____ .

2. J'identifie les mots
familiers et les mots-amis.

_____

_____

_____

3. Je fais une prédiction.
C'est

_____ .

**Est-ce que ma prédiction
est juste?**

Nom : _____ Date : _____

Je fais des prédictions. _____

Avant de lire le texte, je fais des prédictions.

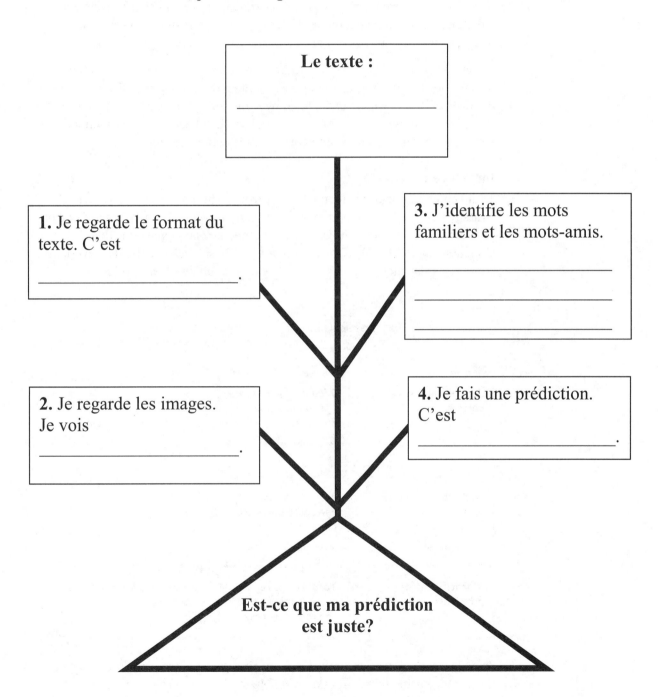

Le texte :

_____

1. Je regarde le format du texte. C'est

_____ .

3. J'identifie les mots familiers et les mots-amis.

_____

_____

_____

2. Je regarde les images. Je vois

_____ .

4. Je fais une prédiction. C'est

_____ .

Est-ce que ma prédiction est juste?

3. Monitor and Repair Comprehension:

Je vérifie ma compréhension.

As FSL teachers, we are aware that texts present challenges for our students due to their limited knowledge of French. When we explore texts with the class, we frequently pause and ask students questions to gauge comprehension. If students are unable to respond to comprehension questions or if the responses are not accurate, we repair comprehension by revisiting the text, defining certain words, and emphasizing graphics or other visual cues. We acknowledge that elementary FSL students may respond to some of these questions with key words or phrases rather than complete sentences.

Effective text users are able to monitor or check their own understanding of a text as they listen, view, or read. As students navigate a text in French, we discover that they will be challenged by some texts because they do not immediately understand all of the vocabulary they hear or see. Students need strategies in order to check and correct their understanding.

Introduce the Strategy

To aid comprehension, students benefit from a simple explanation of the strategy that they are going to use. This can be done by displaying a visual or several visuals for the strategy, illustrating the key language cues that students may use to talk about the strategy. These cues may be displayed on strategy cards, anchor charts, or on acetates for an overhead projector.

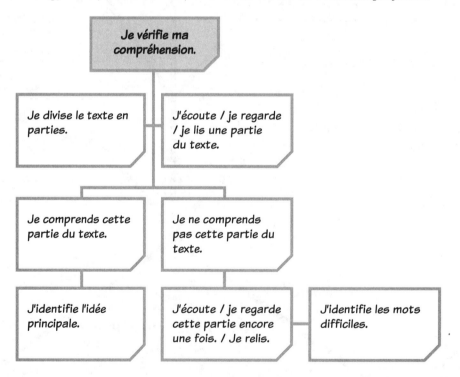

Since learning to use a strategy is an ongoing process, frequent references to the strategy using different texts will help students internalize its use. Consider introducing one language cue at a time to make strategy lessons short and simple. In this way, students will develop a repertoire of language cues and strategies over the course of the school year.

Model the Strategy

In order to effectively monitor their understanding of text, students rely on a variety of tools. When teachers use a Think Aloud to model these tools, this strategy becomes more explicit.

Practise the Strategy

During the exploration of a text, teachers suggest ways to determine students' level of understanding and to help them enhance their understanding. After listening to, viewing, or reading a chunk of text, students can try to put the information into their own words. Students may choose to use only key words if they do not have the vocabulary required to respond in full sentences.

See model language for Think Aloud, Shared and Guided Practice, and Reflection, pp. 86–88.

See Fiche d'activité 3 : Je vérifie ma compréhension, p. 89.

To simplify:	To add challenge:
• Ask students to underline the part of the text that expresses the main idea and help students find the key words in the sections they have underlined. – *Soulignez l'idée principale.* – *Encerclez les mots importants.* • Ask students to listen to a very short part of the text. Then have them recall some of the key words or the main idea from that section that they have heard. Ask students to orally repeat this information.	• Ask students to write a short sentence expressing the main idea. – *Quelle est l'idée principale?* – *Écrivez une phrase.*

Reflect on the Strategy

Students may complete a flow chart as they work through the steps of this strategy. To aid with reflection, it may be helpful for teachers to complete two anchor charts with the class, identifying steps to follow when students understand a chunk of text and steps to follow when they don't.

Assessment for Learning

Do students...

• pause and ask themselves questions?

• put new text into their own words?

• use text features, such as titles and visuals, and familiar words to monitor and repair understanding?

• use a personal dictionary and other resources to look up unfamiliar and new words?

Model Language
Monitor and Repair Comprehension: *Je vérifie ma compréhension.*

In the following examples, students are exploring the theme of heroes. The teacher Thinks Aloud as the class listens to, views, or reads a text in which young people are identifying qualities they admire in their heroes.

Modelling
Moi, je le fais; vous, vous observez.

Think Aloud: Aural, Visual, and Written Text

Je comprends cette partie du texte.

- *Je divise le texte en parties.*
- *J'écoute / je regarde / je lis une partie du texte. Est-ce que je comprends?*
- *Oui, je comprends cette partie du texte.*
- *J'identifie l'idée principale.*
- *L'idée principale est «Ma grand-mère est mon héroïne.»*
- *Je continue.*

Je ne comprends pas cette partie du texte.

- *J'écoute / je regarde / je lis une deuxième partie du texte. Est-ce que je comprends?*
- *Hmm… Non, je ne comprends pas cette partie tu texte.*
- *J'arrête. J'écoute / je regarde / je lis cette partie encore une fois.*
- *J'identifie les mots familiers et les mots-amis.*
- *«Intelligent» est un mot-ami et «joueur» est un mot familier.*
- *J'identifie les mots difficiles.*
- *Les mots difficiles sont «gentil» et «honnête». Je cherche ces mots dans mon dictionnaire.*
- *J'identifie le contexte.*
- *C'est une description. Je regarde dans ma banque de vocabulaire.*
- *Ah, maintenant, je comprends. L'idée principale est «Wayne Gretzky est un héros.»*

Shared Practice: Aural, Visual, and Written Text

Je comprends cette partie du texte.

- *Je divise le texte en parties.*
- *J'écoute / je regarde / je lis une partie du texte.*
- *Est-ce que je comprends? (Oui, je comprends cette partie du texte.)*
- *J'identifie l'idée principale. (L'idée principale est _____.)*
- *Je continue.*

Je ne comprends pas cette partie du texte.

- *J'écoute / je regarde / je lis une deuxième partie du texte. Est-ce que je comprends?*
- *Non, je ne comprends pas.*
- *J'arrête. J'écoute / je regarde / je lis cette partie encore une fois.*
- *J'identifie les mots familiers et les mots-amis. (_____ est un mot familier et _____ est un mot-ami.)*
- *J'identifie les mots difficiles. (Les mots difficiles sont _____ et _____.)*
- *J'utilise le contexte. (_____.)*
- *Maintenant, je comprends.*

Guided Practice: Aural, Visual, and Written Text

Je comprends cette partie du texte.

- *Qu'est-ce que vous faites en premier? (Je divise le texte en parties.)*
- *Très bien. Écoutez / regardez / lisez cette partie du texte.*
- *Bravo! Vous comprenez? (Oui, je comprends. / Non, je ne comprends pas.)*
- *Vous comprenez, bravo! Qu'est-ce que vous faites maintenant? (J'identifie l'idée principale.)*
- *Très bien. Et quelle est l'idée principale? (L'idée principale est _____.)*

Je ne comprends pas cette partie du texte.

- *Vous ne comprenez pas. Alors, nous allons écouter / regarder / relire cette partie encore une fois.*
- *Qu'est-ce que vous faites maintenant? (J'identifie les mots familiers et les mots-amis.)*
- *C'est ça. Et quels sont les mots familiers et les mots-amis? (_____ est un mot-ami et _____ est un mot familier.)*
- *Qu'est-ce que vous faites ensuite? (J'identifie les mots difficiles.)*
- *Super! Et quels sont les mots difficiles? (Les mots difficiles sont _____ et _____.)*
- *Qu'est-ce que vous faites pour comprendre les mots difficiles? (J'identifie le contexte.)*
- *Et quel est le contexte? (_____.)*
- *Maintenant, est-ce que vous comprenez?*

Reflection: Aural, Visual, and Written Text

- *Est-ce que je comprends ce texte?*
- *Qu'est-ce que je fais pour comprendre le texte?*

Écoutons! Regardons! Lisons!

Je vérifie ma compréhension.

☐ **Je divise le texte en parties.**

☐ **J'écoute / Je regarde / Je lis une partie du texte.**

A   **B**

☐ **Je comprends cette partie du texte.**   ou   ☐ **Je ne comprends pas cette partie du texte.**

☐ J'identifie les mots importants.

Les mots importants sont

_____

_____ .

☐ J'écoute / Je regarde cette partie encore une fois. / Je relis.

☐ J'identifie le titre, les images et le contexte.
• Le titre est

_____ .

• Je vois

_____ .

• Le contexte est

_____ .

☐ J'identifie l'idée principale. Cest

_____

_____ .

Je continue!

☐ J'identifie les mots difficiles.

Les mots difficiles sont

_____

_____ .

89 | effective literacy practices in **FSL: making connections**
© Pearson Education Canada Inc.   Fiche d'activité 3

4. Make Connections: *Je fais des liens.*

As students explore text, they develop the ability to link a new text to what they already know. Students' knowledge about themselves, the world (e.g., family, friends, school, local community), and other texts offer them three broad areas to which they may connect a text: text to self, text to world, and text to text. In addition, FSL students may make connections between a text in French and their first language.

When students connect prior knowledge about themselves, the world, or other texts to a current text, they are more likely to focus on and remember new content. For example, if students read e-mail messages from students in another province, they will connect the information about what these students like to do with activities they do in their local community. If a student is watching a video in which young people are describing fundraising projects in their local community, the student may associate this text with a current fundraising campaign happening at his or her school. A student's prior knowledge serves as a kind of filter or lens through which new information is viewed. This prior knowledge allows the student to see the new information more clearly and to situate it within existing knowledge, so that it may be understood and remembered.

Introduce the Strategy

To aid comprehension, students benefit from a simple explanation of the strategy that they are going to use. This can be done by displaying a visual or several visuals for the strategy, illustrating the key language cues that students may use to talk about the strategy. These cues may be displayed on strategy cards, anchor charts, or on acetates for an overhead projector.

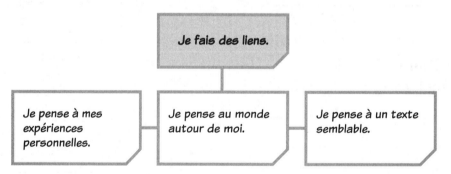

Since learning to use a strategy is an ongoing process, frequent references to the strategy using different texts will help students internalize its use. Consider introducing one language cue at a time to make strategy lessons short and simple. In this way, students will develop a repertoire of language cues and strategies over the course of the school year.

Model the Strategy

Teachers may wish to set the context by reviewing some of the pre-reading questions used in the "Ask Questions" strategy to remind students of the connections the text has to their own personal experiences. Help students ask questions that will assist them in making connections between the text and themselves, the world, and / or other texts.

See model language for Think Aloud, Shared and Guided Practice, and Reflection, p. 92.

It is important to encourage students to make connections between the text and their first language or other subject areas. For example, as students think about the new text, they may realize that they have experience with similar texts in English, or that the topic relates to something they are studying in their Social Studies or Language Arts class. Integrating the new text and what they do in FSL class with other subjects will help to enhance their understanding and appreciation for the text.

Practise the Strategy

Using a graphic organizer, students record how a text connects to their personal experiences, the world, and / or other texts. They may take the sentences directly from the text or use sentence starters to help write sentences about what they already know. Students who experience difficulty may be given the option to draw an image or use key words in their responses. The teacher may also provide some key words from which the student may choose to respond.

See Fiche d'activité 4 : Je fais des liens, p. 93.

To simplify:	To add challenge:
• Ask students to underline words that they recognize and that connect to their prior learning. – *Identifiez les mots familiers et les mots-amis.* • Encourage students to draw a picture rather than write their responses. – *Dessinez l'idée principale.* – *Dessinez vos liens.*	• Ask students to bring in an artifact from home that is connected to the text, share it with the class, and briefly explain the link. – *Trouvez un objet à la maison associé avec le texte. Présentez cet objet à un(e) partenaire.*

Reflect on the Strategy

Identifying the links made to a text is important, but it is equally important that students be given the opportunity to talk about those links with their classmates. Students may share the ideas on their graphic organizer with one or more partners. Teachers may then encourage them to talk about similarities in a large group setting.

Assessment for Learning

Do students...
• make logical connections to the text?
• make connections between text and self, text and the world, text and text?

Model Language
Make Connections: *Je fais des liens.*

In the following examples, students explore the topic of pastimes. They may listen to a text in which other young people are describing their pastimes, view a video about people and their pastimes, or read about unusual pastimes.

Modelling
Moi, je le fais; vous, vous observez.

Think Aloud: Aural, Visual, and Written Text

- *J'écoute / je regarde / je lis le texte.*
- *J'identifie l'idée principale.*
- *Eh bien, l'idée principale est «Marc adore jouer au hockey.»*
- *Maintenant, je fais des liens.*
- *En premier, je pense à mes expériences personnelles.*
- *Hmm… Moi, j'aime regarder un match de hockey à la télé.*
- *Ensuite, je pense au monde autour de moi.*
- *Ah! Dans ma famille, mon frère adore jouer au hockey.*
- *Et troisièmement, je pense à un texte semblable.*
- *Le livre «The Hockey Book for Girls» par Stacey Wilson est semblable.*

Shared Practice
Moi, je le fais; vous, vous m'aidez.

Shared Practice: Aural, Visual, and Written Text

- *J'écoute / je regarde / je lis le texte.*
- *J'identifie l'idée principale. (C'est _____.)*
- *Maintenant, je fais des liens.*
- *En premier, je pense à mes expériences personnelles. (Moi, je _____.)*
- *Ensuite, je pense au monde autour de moi. (Dans _____, _____.)*
- *Troisièmement, je pense à un texte semblable. (Le texte _____ est semblable.)*

Guided Practice
Toi et ton ami(e), vous le faites; moi, je vous aide.

Independent Practice
Vous, vous le faites; moi, j'observe.

Guided Practice: Aural, Visual, and Written Text

- *Écoutez / regardez / lisez le texte et faites des liens.*
- *Qu'est-ce que vous faites en premier? (J'identifie l'idée principale.)*
- *Très bien. Quelle est l'idée principale? (C'est _____.)*
- *Et ensuite? (Je pense à mes expériences personnelles.)*
- *Quelles sont vos expériences personnelles? (Moi, je _____.)*
- *Et ensuite? (Je pense au monde autour de moi).*
- *C'est ça. Qu'est-ce qui se passe dans le monde autour de vous? (Dans _____, _____.)*
- *Et troisièmement? (Je pense à un texte semblable.)*
- *Parfait. Quel texte est semblable? (Le texte _____ est semblable.)*

Reflection: Aural, Visual, and Written Text

- *Comparez votre fiche avec la fiche d'un(e) partenaire. Quels liens sont semblables?*

Nom : _____ Date : _____

Je fais des liens.

Je note mes liens avec le texte.

J'identifie l'idée principale.

_____

_____

Je pense à mes expériences personnelles.

- à mes préférences
- à mes classes
- à mes activités

_____

_____

Je pense à un texte semblable.

- à un livre
- à un film

_____

_____

Je pense au monde autour de moi.

- à ma famille
- à mes amis
- à la télé et à l'Internet

_____

_____

5. Visualize: *Je vois une image dans ma tête.*

Visualizing means creating a mental image of a message to bring the text to life and make it more vivid. In FSL, students rely on visual images to help fill in some of the gaps when they read and encounter unfamiliar words. Creating a mental image, while exploring a text, helps the student become engaged and remain motivated. Vivid visualization also helps students recall details and enhances the enjoyment of the experience.

After students have created a mental image, they may draw some simple conclusions about a text they have listened to, viewed, or read. For example, as students explore a text about activities, they may visualize young people playing hockey, rock climbing, or cycling, and suggest that they are *sportifs* or *sportives*. Similarly, they may conclude that young people playing piano, painting, or dancing are *créatifs* or *créatives*.

Introduce the Strategy

To aid comprehension, students benefit from a simple explanation of the strategy that they are going to use. This can be done by displaying a visual or several visuals for the strategy, illustrating the key language cues that students may use to talk about the strategy. These cues may be displayed on strategy cards, anchor charts, or on acetates for an overhead projector.

Since learning to use a strategy is an ongoing process, frequent references to the strategy using different texts will help students internalize its use. Consider introducing one language cue at a time to make strategy lessons short and simple. In this way, students will develop a repertoire of language cues and strategies over the course of the school year.

Model the Strategy

To help students identify key elements in a text, teachers Think Aloud as they model the visualization strategy, then draw conclusions about what they see.

Practise the Strategy

Engage students in a visualization activity that places them in the text. Have them pause and close their eyes after they listen to, view, or read a manageable chunk of text. Ask students to draw what they visualize by focusing on the key words from the text.

See model language for Think Aloud, Shared and Guided Practice, and Reflection, p. 96.

See Fiche d'activité 5 : Je dessine une image, p. 97.

Once students have an image of a particular chunk of text, the teacher may prompt them to draw conclusions, or make observations about the theme, character or setting. This may be challenging for elementary FSL students, but inferences can be very simple, such as asking students how a character might be feeling in a certain situation or by selecting an adjective to describe a character according to what he or she does or says.

To simplify:	To add challenge:
• Offer students a choice of responses to questions to help them make observations. – *Est-ce que cette personne est triste ou contente?* – *Est-ce que cette personne est active ou tranquille?*	• Ask students to explain the reason for their observations. – *Selon vous, cette personne est triste. Quels sont les indices? (Comment est-ce que vous savez?)*

Reflect on the Strategy

Once students have completed their visualization activity, they may compare their drawings and observations with one or more classmates. Teachers may need to provide students with sentence starters or models to enable them to verbalize the similarities and differences in their drawings.

Assessment for Learning

Do students...
• look at the images and relate them to the text?
• sketch an image from the text that reflects key messages from the text?
• make some observations or draw some conclusions about the text?

Model Language
Visualize: *Je vois une image dans ma tête.*

In the following examples, students explore favourite foods. They listen to conversations between students who talk about where they like to eat, view a TV commercial about food, or read a menu for a popular fast-food restaurant.

Modelling
Moi, je le fais; vous, vous observez.

Think Aloud: Aural Text, Visual, and Written Text

- *J'écoute / je regarde / je lis un texte.*
- *J'identifie les mots familiers et les mots-amis.*
- *Hmm… Les mots familiers et les mots-amis sont «la casse-croûte, manger, les pitas».*
- *J'écoute / je regarde encore une fois. / Je relis.*
- *Je vois une image dans ma tête.*
- *Eh bien, je vois des amis. Je vois une casse-croûte.*
- *Je dessine une image.*
- *Ah! Je dessine la table et les amis. Ils mangent des pitas.*
- *Je fais des observations.*
- *Hmm… Les amis adorent les pitas.*

Shared Practice
Moi, je le fais; et vous, vous m'aidez.

Shared Practice: Aural, Visual, and Written Text

- *J'écoute / je regarde / je lis un texte.*
- *J'identifie les mots familiers et les mots-amis. (Les mots familiers et les mots-amis sont _____.)*
- *J'écoute / je regarde encore une fois. / Je relis.*
- *Je vois une image dans ma tête. (Je vois _____.)*
- *Je dessine une image. (Je dessine _____.)*
- *Je fais des observations. (_____.)*

Guided Practice
Toi et ton ami(e), vous le faites; moi, je vous aide.

Independent Practice
Vous, vous le faites; moi, j'observe.

Guided Practice: Aural, Visual, and Written Text

- *Écoutez / regardez / lisez le texte.*
- *Qu'est-ce que vous faites en premier? (J'identifie les mots familiers et les mots-amis.)*
- *Quels sont les mots familiers et les mots-amis? (Les mots familiers et les mots-amis sont _____ et _____.)*
- *Écoutez / regardez le texte encore une fois. / Relisez.*
- *Qu'est-ce que vous faites maintenant? (Je vois une image dans ma tête.)*
- *Parfait! Qu'est-ce que vous voyez? (Je vois _____.)*
- *Et ensuite? (Je dessine une image.)*
- *Excellent! Qu'est-ce que vous dessinez? (Je dessine _____.)*
- *Qu'est-ce que vous faites après? (Je fais des observations.)*
- *C'est ça. Qu'est-ce que vous observez? (_____.)*

Reflection: Aural, Visual, and Written Text

- *Comparez votre image avec l'image de votre partenaire. Quelles images sont semblables? Quelles images sont différentes?*
- *Comparez vos observations. Est-ce que vos observations sont semblables?*

Nom : _____Date : _____   **Fiche d'activité 5**

Je dessine une image.

A. Voici les mots importants.

_____   _____

_____   _____

B. Je vois une image dans ma tête. Voici mon image.

[empty box]

C. Je fais une observation.

_____

6. Summarize: *J'identifie l'idée principale.*

When students summarize what they have learned in a text, they draw on all of the other skills they have used to work with the text thus far. This can be challenging for elementary FSL students because their vocabulary is limited. It is a skill students use more readily in a first language setting because they have a large repertoire of words to paraphrase what they have understood in a text. In an FSL setting, students may start by searching for and copying key phrases from the text. They distinguish between the main ideas and the supporting details, and may also draw some conclusions.

The use of graphic organizers, such as charts, webs, and timelines, is helpful for students to extract key ideas or information, thus highlighting what they have read and understood. Representing this visually allows students to feel a sense of accomplishment about their level of comprehension.

Introduce the Strategy

To aid comprehension, students benefit from a simple explanation of the strategy that they are going to use. This can be done by displaying a visual or several visuals for the strategy, illustrating the key language cues that students may use to talk about the strategy. These cues may be displayed on strategy cards, anchor charts, or on acetates for an overhead projector.

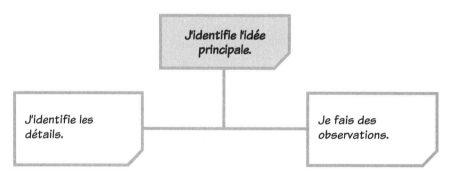

Since learning to use a strategy is an ongoing process, frequent references to the strategy using different texts will help students internalize its use. Consider introducing one language cue at a time to make strategy lessons short and simple. In this way, students will develop a repertoire of language cues and strategies over the course of the school year.

Model the Strategy

Teachers may have students consider the events or ideas they have just explored in a text. They may have already used one or more strategies with the text, such as asking questions, making predictions, monitoring comprehension, making connections, or visualizing. They are now ready to summarize what they have understood.

Students may learn to use this strategy with a narrative text, whereby a sequence of events tells a story, or with an informative text, whereby ideas may be organized according to categories. Using a Think Aloud, the teacher shows students how to identify the main ideas, distinguish between the main ideas and supporting details, and look for connections between ideas in the text.

See model language for Think Aloud, Shared and Guided Practice, and Reflection, pp. 100–101

Practise the Strategy

Have students note the key ideas from the text either in a sequence (i.e., a narrative text) or in categories (i.e., an informative text).

See Fiche d'activité 6 : J'identifie les idées principales, p. 102.

See Fiche d'activité 7 : J'organise les idées, p. 103.

To simplify:	To add challenge:
• Ask students to plot the events in a narrative text by recording key phrases or sentences along a timeline. – *Écrivez une phrase ou des mots pour chaque événement dans le texte sur une ligne de temps.* • Ask students to record all titles and subtitles in an informative text. Ask them to record one key phrase for each of these main ideas. – *Écrivez les titres et sous-titres dans le texte.* – *Écrivez une phrase ou des mots pour chaque titre ou idée.* • Ask clarifying questions to differentiate between main ideas and supporting details. – *Est-ce que c'est une idée principale ou est-ce que cette idée est moins importante?*	• Ask students to identify the cues that point to the most important ideas. – *Selon vous, pourquoi est-ce que cette idée est l'idée principale? (Le titre est gros. L'idée est dans le premier paragraphe. Il y a une photo qui va avec l'idée.)* • Ask students to explain how the text is organized and how the text could be organized differently. – *Comment est-ce que le texte est organisé? (Il y a une photo / un sous-titre pour chaque événement.)* – *Comment est-ce que vous pouvez organiser ce texte d'une façon différente? (Je peux organiser les événements par province.)* • Ask students to make connections between categories or clusters of ideas. Ask them if they see links to details in other areas of the text. – *Est-ce qu'il y a des liens dans le texte? (Trois événements ont de la nourriture spéciale. Deux des événements ont un défilé.)*

Reflect on the Strategy

Teachers may have students compare how they have organized the main ideas or linked the ideas from the text, because not everyone will have approached this in the same way.

Assessment for Learning

Do students...
• select key ideas rather than details in summarizing the text?
• support their choices by noticing how the author has emphasized or linked certain ideas in the text?
• record the key ideas in a logical sequence?
• link ideas to others in a logical way?

Model Language for Narrative Text
Summarize: *J'identifie l'idée principale.*

In the following examples, students explore a narrative text about special events. They read a narrative story about two friends attending a blueberry festival in Québec.

Modelling
Moi, je le fais; vous, vous observez.

Think Aloud: Narrative Text

- *Je lis le texte.*
- ***J'identifie l'idée principale et les détails.***
- *Eh bien, au début Mira et Saul vont au Festival du bleuet.*
- ***Et les détails...*** *C'est le mois d'août. Il fait chaud.*
- ***Et ensuite?***
- *Ah, Mira et Saul mangent de la tarte au bleuet.*
- ***Et les détails...*** *C'est une tarte géante!*
- ***Et à la fin?***
- *Hmm, Mira et Saul mangent trop.*
- *Ah! Ils sont malades. C'est dommage!*
- ***Je fais des observations.***
- *Hmm... toutes les décorations pour le festival sont bleues.*

Shared Practice: Narrative Text

- *Je lis le texte.*
- *J'identifie l'idée principale et les détails. (Au début, Mira et Saul vont _____.)*
- *Et les détails? (C'est _____.)*
- *Et l'idée principale ensuite... (Mira et Saul mangent _____.)*
- *Et les détails? (C'est _____.)*
- *À la fin? (Mira et Saul _____.)*
- *Et les détails? (Ils sont _____.)*
- *Je fais des observations. (_____.)*

Shared Practice
Moi, je le fais; et vous, vous m'aidez.

Guided Practice: Narrative Text

- *Relisez le texte.*
- *Qu'est-ce que vous faites en premier? (J'identifie l'idée principale.)*
- *Et ensuite? (J'identifie les détails.)*
- *Excellent. Quelle est l'idée principale au début? (_____.)*
- *Et ensuite? (_____.)*
- *Et à la fin? (_____.)*
- *C'est ça. Et quels sont les détails au début? (_____.)*
- *Et ensuite? (_____.)*
- *Et à la fin? (_____.)*
- *Qu'est-ce que vous faites après? (Je fais des observations.)*
- *Très bien. Qu'est-ce que vous observez? (_____.)*

Guided Practice
Toi et ton ami(e), vous le faites; moi, je vous aide.

Independent Practice
Vous, vous le faites; moi, j'observe.

Model Language for Informative Text
Summarize: *J'identifie l'idée principale.*

In the following examples, students explore an informative text about events. They watch a video and learn about the location, dates, main features, and interesting details about several special events celebrated across the country.

Think Aloud: Informative Text

- *Je regarde la vidéo.*
- *J'identifie l'idée principale.*
- *Hmm… L'idée principale est «Il y a des événements au Canada.»*
- *J'identifie les détails.*
- *Ah! C'est le Stampede de Calgary. La date : Le Stampede est en juillet. Des activités spéciales : Il y a un défilé.*
- *Je fais des observations.*
- *Tous les événements ont des compétitions.*

Modelling
Moi, je le fais; vous, vous observez.

Shared Practice: Informative Text

- *Je regarde la vidéo.*
- *J'identifie l'idée principale. (Il y a des _____.)*
- *J'identifie les détails. (C'est _____. L'endroit : _____. La date : _____. La musique : _____. Les costumes : _____. Des activités spéciales : _____.)*
- *Je fais des observations. (Tous les événements _____.)*

Shared Practice
Moi, je le fais; vous, vous m'aidez.

Guided Practice: Informative Text

- *Regardez la vidéo encore une fois.*
- *Qu'est-ce que vous faites en premier? (J'identifie l'idée principale.)*
- *Excellent. Quelle est l'idée principale? (L'idée principale est _____.)*
- *Et ensuite? (J'identifie les détails.)*
- *C'est ça. Quels sont les détails? (_____.)*
- *Qu'est-ce que vous faites maintenant? (Je fais des observations.)*
- *Très bien. Qu'est-ce que vous observez? (_____.)*

Guided Practice
Toi et ton ami(e), vous le faites; moi, je vous aide.

Independent Practice
Vous, vous le faites; moi, j'observe.

Reflection: Aural, Visual, and Written Text (Narrative and Information Text)

- *Comparez votre fiche avec la fiche de votre partenaire.*
- *Selon vous, quelle est l'idée principale? Comparez votre réponse à la réponse de votre partenaire.*
- *Est-ce que vous avez les mêmes idées que votre partenaire?*

Écoutons!   Regardons!   Lisons!

Nom : _____ Date : _____

J'identifie les idées principales.

A. Je note les idées principales. Je dessine les détails.

Au début…

    1. _____

       _____

       _____

Ensuite…

    2. _____

       _____

       _____

À la fin…

    3. _____

       _____

       _____

B. Je compare mes idées avec les idées d'un ou d'une partenaire.

Écoutons!   Regardons!   Lisons!

Nom :_____ Date : _____   Fiche d'activité 7

J'organise les idées.

A. Je note les idées principales et les détails. Je dessine des images.

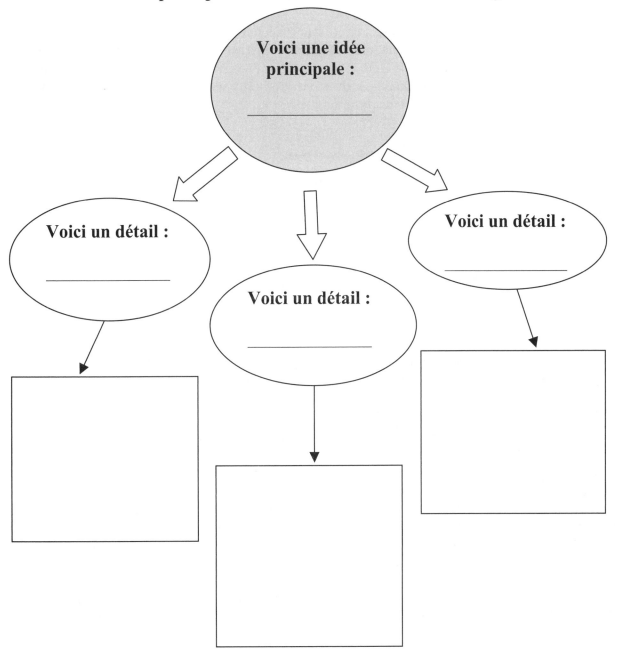

Voici une idée principale :

_____

Voici un détail :

_____

Voici un détail :

_____

Voici un détail :

_____

B. Je compare mes idées avec les idées d'un ou d'une partenaire.

Fiche d'activité 7

7. Synthesize: *Je fais la synthèse.*

When students synthesize a text, they go beyond retelling facts or storylines. They start by thinking about what they have learned in the text and connect this to information and ideas they have learned in other texts or in the world in general. They reorganize and transform the ideas and information into a new form that demonstrates their understanding. FSL students use a variety of formats to present this information, just as they would in first language classrooms.

Introduce the Strategy

To aid comprehension, students benefit from a simple explanation of the strategy that they are going to use. This can be done by displaying a visual or several visuals for the strategy, illustrating the key language cues that students may use to talk about the strategy. These cues may be displayed on strategy cards, anchor charts, or on acetates for an overhead projector.

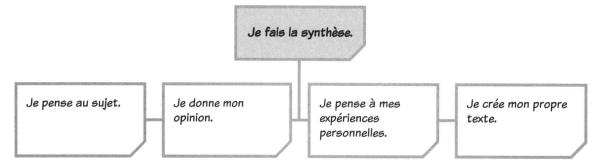

Since learning to use a strategy is an ongoing process, frequent references to the strategy using different texts will help students internalize its use. Consider introducing one language cue at a time to make strategy lessons short and simple. In this way, students will develop a repertoire of language cues and strategies over the course of the school year.

Model the Strategy

See model language for Think Aloud, Shared and Guided Practice, and Reflection, p. 106.

Teachers Think Aloud to review the key ideas already identified in the text. What are the main ideas in the text? What connections do I bring to this topic? What is my opinion on the topic? What aspect of the topic interests me the most? Teachers show students how to process these questions and answers and how to enhance their learning with information related to the main ideas of the text. This may involve drawing from background knowledge, consulting other sources, or conducting research—for example, checking a simple French Web site previewed by the teacher, consulting another French text on the same topic, or conducting an in-class survey. It is important to model how to draw out these questions using language that is accessible to students yet that allows them to represent what they understand.

Practise the Strategy

Students may use a graphic organizer to record one or more main ideas in the text. First, invite students to add a personal interpretation of the text's topics by giving their opinion and choosing an idea that they would like to develop. Students may choose to present their idea in a variety of ways. Some texts and representations may lend themselves to animation in a skit, demonstration, or multimedia format. Encourage students to add graphic or illustrative touches to their work.

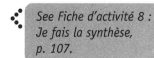

See Fiche d'activité 8 : Je fais la synthèse, p. 107.

To simplify:	**To add challenge:**
• Provide sentence starters that help students represent what they have learned in the text. – *J'apprends de nouvelles choses :* _____. – *Dans ce texte, il y a cinq sports extrêmes. Ils sont* _____. • Ask students to rank the sports presented in the text according to one of several criteria provided, such as, *C'est le sport le plus difficile. C'est le sport le plus amusant.* They should record one sentence from the text about each sport. – *Donnez votre opinion. Choisissez une description pour chaque sport.*	• Ask students to explain their opinion by completing their sentence with *parce que.* – *J'aime / je n'aime pas / je préfère* _____ *parce que* _____. • Ask students to list questions about the topic that are of interest to them. The answers to these questions are not necessarily found in the text. Then ask them to identify sources of information for their questions. – *Est-ce que vous avez d'autres questions sur les sports extrêmes? (Qui fait ces sports au Canada? Quels records existent pour chaque sport?)* – *Où est-ce que vous trouvez les réponses à vos questions? (Je trouve de l'information dans un livre, dans un site Web, à la télé.)*

Reflect on the Strategy

Have students share their representations. Invite them to notice how different students have focused on certain ideas or information. Encourage students to give feedback to peers about the ideas they have added.

Assessment for Learning

Do students...

• represent additional information in a logical and/or meaningful way?
• add their own idea(s) to this representation?
• consult other texts to add information or ideas related to the text's theme? (optional)

Model Language
Synthesize: *Je fais la synthèse.*

In the following examples, students have explored texts about extreme sports. They have listened to, viewed, and read informative texts about some new and exciting extreme sports.

Modelling
Moi, je le fais; vous, vous observez.

> **Think Aloud: Aural , Visual, and Written Text**
>
> - **Je pense au sujet.**
> - **Je donne mon opinion.**
> - *Eh bien, moi, j'aime les sports sur terre.*
> - **Je pense à mes expériences personnelles.**
> - *Je sais! Moi, j'aime faire du vélo.*
> - **Je crée mon propre texte.**
> - *Je crée un diagramme.*

Shared Practice
Moi, je le fais; vous, vous m'aidez.

> **Shared Practice: Aural, Visual, and Written Text**
>
> - *Je pense au sujet.*
> - *Je donne mon opinion. (J'aime / je n'aime pas / je préfère _____.)*
> - *Je pense à mes expériences personnelles. (J'aime _____.)*
> - *Je crée mon propre texte. (Je crée _____.)*
>
> **Guided Practice: Aural, Visual, and Written Text**
>
> - *Qu'est-ce que vous faites en premier? (Je pense au sujet. Je donne mon opinion.)*
> - *Excellent. Quelle est votre opinion? (J'aime / je n'aime pas / je préfère _____.)*
> - *Qu'est-ce que vous faites ensuite? (Je pense à mes expériences personelles.)*
> - *Oui. Quelles sont vos expériences personnelles? (J'aime _____.)*
> - *Qu'est-ce que vous faites ensuite? (Je crée mon propre texte.)*
> - *Qu'est-ce que vous créez comme texte? (Je crée _____.)*

Guided Practice
Toi et ton ami(e), vous le faites; moi, je vous aide.

Independent Practice
Vous, vous le faites; moi, j'observe.

> **Reflection: Aural, Visual, and Written Text**
>
> - *Quelles informations sont nouvelles pour vous?*
> - *Donnez votre opinion sur ce sujet.*
> - *Comparez vos idées avec les idées des autres élèves. Est-ce que vos idées sont semblables ou différentes?*

Nom : _____   Date : _____

Je fais la synthèse.

A. Je pense au sujet.

1. J'identifie le sujet du texte.

_____

_____

2. Je donne mon opinion.

☐ J'aime _____.

☐ Je n'aime pas _____.

☐ Je suis d'accord. / Je ne suis pas d'accord.

3. Je pense à mes expériences personnelles.

☐ Je pense à _____.

☐ Je veux parler de _____.

☐ Cet aspect du sujet m'intéresse :
_____.

B. Je crée mon propre texte.

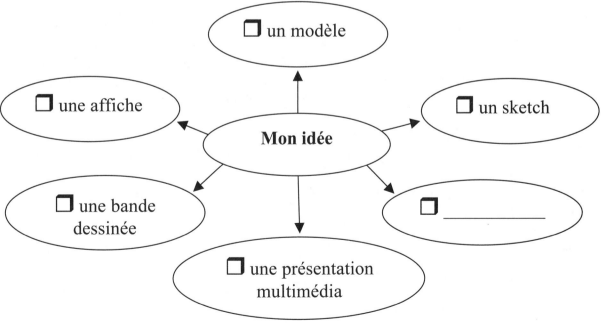

☐ un modèle

☐ une affiche

Mon idée

☐ un sketch

☐ une bande dessinée

☐ _____

☐ une présentation multimédia

After

8. Analyse and Evaluate: *Je réfléchis.*

After exploring a text, it is time for students to think about it in terms of what matters to them. They have focused on the important ideas in the text and linked them to other ideas and information. Students must now consider what difference the text has made to them personally. This is an important step in becoming critical text users.

When able to do so, students may also consider how the author has presented the text's content, organized the text, emphasized certain aspects and not others, used certain features to enhance meaning or understanding, and so on. The challenge for FSL students (and their teachers) is to engage in this deeper consideration of text in ways that are personally meaningful yet linguistically feasible.

Introduce the Strategy

To aid comprehension, students benefit from a simple explanation of the strategy they are going to use. This can be done by displaying a visual or several visuals for the strategy, illustrating the key language cues that students may use to talk about the strategy. These cues may be displayed on strategy cards, anchor charts, or on acetates for an overhead projector.

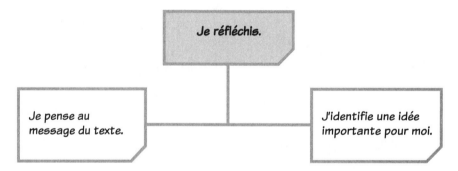

Je réfléchis.

Je pense au message du texte.

J'identifie une idée importante pour moi.

Since learning to use a strategy is an ongoing process, frequent references to the strategy using different texts will help students internalize its use. Consider introducing one language cue at a time to make strategy lessons short and simple. In this way, students will develop a repertoire of language cues and strategies over the course of the school year.

Model the Strategy

In a Think Aloud, teachers model how students may reflect on the ideas in the text. What will they remember? What lessons will they take forward? This exploration is more possible with some texts than others.

See model language for Think Aloud, Shared and Guided Practice, and Reflection, p. 110.

Practise the Strategy

Teachers may ask students to use a journal to record their personal response to the text, note the key ideas or message, and make some observations about questions that were and were not addressed in the text. This may be conducted as an individual activity or as a collaborative task where the class participates orally, and the teacher scribes, to produce a group response.

See Fiche d'activité 9 : Mon journal, p. 111.

To simplify:	To add challenge:
• Provide possible responses for student reflections. – *Le message du texte est...* ❑ *Les collections originales sont importantes.* ❑ *Les amis montrent leur collection à leurs amis.* ❑ *Toutes les collections sont intéressantes.* – *Une idée importante pour moi est...* ❑ *Je veux une collection unique.* ❑ *Je garde ma collection dans une boîte.* ❑ *Je parle de ma collection avec mes amis.*	• Ask students to make observations about how the author has structured the text or organized the ideas. Students may comment on how the author has treated the theme, for example, by emphasizing certain aspects, using repetition, and so on. – *Comment est-ce que l'auteur a organisé le texte? (L'auteur répète les idées importantes, etc.)* • Students may share their responses with other students who have explored the same text (via a book rap) or with the text's author. – *Comparez vos commentaires avec les commentaires d'un ou d'une partenaire.* – *Avez-vous des questions ou des commentaires pour l'auteur?*

Reflect on the Strategy

Have students share their personal responses to the text.

Assessment for Learning

Do students...
• identify a central message or lesson?
• provide a personal response to the text?

Model Language
Analyse and Evaluate: *Je réfléchis.*

In the following examples, students have explored a text on extraordinary and unique collections. They talk about and share their own collections, and present their collections to the class after summarizing the key points from the text (and perhaps consulting other texts). They are now ready to reflect on their experience with the text(s).

Modelling
Moi, je le fais; vous, vous observez.

Think Aloud: Aural, Visual, and Written Text

- ***Je réfléchis.***

- ***Je pense au message du texte.***

- *Eh bien, le message du texte est «Beaucoup de personnes ont des collections originales.»*

- ***J'identifie une idée importante pour moi.***

- *Hmm… Je garde ma collection dans une boîte.*

Shared Practice
Moi, je le fais; vous, vous m'aidez.

Shared Practice: Aural, Visual, and Written Text

- *Je réfléchis.*

- *Je pense au message du texte. (_____.)*

- *J'identifie une idée importante pour moi. (_____.)*

Guided Practice
Toi et ton ami(e), vous le faites; moi, je vous aide.

Independent Practice
Vous, vous le faites; moi, j'observe.

Guided Practice: Aural, Visual, and Written Text

- *Réfléchissez.*

- *Qu'est-ce que vous faites en premier? (Je pense au message du texte.)*

- *Très bien. Quel est le message de ce texte? (_____.)*

- *Et ensuite? (J'identifie une idée importante pour moi.)*

- *Bravo! Quelle idée est importante pour vous? (_____.)*

Reflection: Aural, Visual, and Written Text

- *Comparez vos opinions avec un ou une partenaire.*

Nom : _____ Date : _____ Fiche d'activité 9

Mon journal _____

Je pense au sujet.

Le titre du texte : _____

1. Voici le sujet du texte :

_____

_____

2. Voici une idée importante pour moi :

_____

_____

3. Voici un détail qui n'est pas dans le texte :

_____

_____

4. Voici une question ou un commentaire pour l'auteur :

_____

_____

5. Voici un dessin, un symbole ou un logo pour ce texte :

Appendix A:
Tactics and Organizers to Support the Big Ideas

Introduction

During the learning sequence (*before*, *during*, and *after* the exploration of a text), teachers focus on key comprehension strategies and help students take ownership of these processes. The process is not linear; it often requires the learner to go back and rethink, or to shift focus to a different strategy or step.

In using these tactics and organizers, teachers scaffold the learning in order to gradually release responsibility to the students. It is important that some of the tactics are integrated into the context of each lesson sequence.

The following alphabetical list is a partial repertoire of tactics and organizers providing teachers and students with ways and means to make these strategies concrete. The use of these processes with FSL students requires careful scaffolding.

1. AB Partnering
2. Anchor Chart
3. Anticipation Guide
4. Assessment *for* Learning Tools
5. Checklist for Choosing Texts
6. Coding a Text
7. Draw What I Say
8. Fish Bone
9. Flow Chart
10. Inquiry Chart
11. Interview
12. K-W-L and K-W-L Plus Charts
13. Language Games
14. Learning Log/Journal
15. Numbered Heads
16. Place Mat
17. Plus-Minus-Interesting Chart
18. Portfolio
19. Retelling and Role Play
20. Sentence Starters and Models
21. Story Map
22. Timeline
23. Traffic Light
24. Venn Diagram
25. Word Sorts
26. Word Wall/Vocabulary Bank
27. Word Web

1. AB Partnering (*Travail en partenaires*)

AB Partnering is a tactic whereby students are responsible for reporting their partner's information to the class. It is ideal for purposeful oral communication that encourages active listening.

Example: Favourite Activities

In pairs, students ask each other about their favourite activity. The teacher models the question and provides sentence starters. Students are encouraged to use Anchor Charts, Word Walls, and organizers, etc., to help them adapt the model. Through shared and guided practice, students are able to successfully interview a partner. They are then invited to describe their partner's choice to the class.

Shared and Guided Practice

Enseignant(e) : *J'aime écouter de la musique. C'est mon activité préférée.*
Quelle est ton activité préférée?

Élève 1 : *Moi, j'aime <u>jouer au soccer.</u>*

Enseignant(e) : *Et toi, <u>Jessica?</u> Quelle est ton activité préférée?*

Élève 2 : *Moi, j'adore <u>faire du camping.</u>*

Enseignant(e) : *Et toi, <u>Michael?</u> Quelle est ton activité préférée?*

Élève 3 : *J'aime <u>dessiner.</u>*

Model Language
- *Quelle est ton activité préférée?*
- *Moi, j'aime _____.*

Independent Practice

Enseignant(e) : *Maintenant, posez la question à votre partenaire.*

Élève 1 : *Quelle est ton activité préférée?*

Élève 2 : *J'aime _____. Et toi?*

Élève 1 : *J'adore _____.*

Description of their Partner's Choice to the Class

Enseignant(e) : *Nous allons partager les réponses de nos partenaires.*
Jean, qui est ton partenaire?

Jean : *C'est Luc.*

Enseignant(e) : *Quelle est l'activité préférée de Luc?*

Jean : *Il aime _____.*

Enseignant(e) : *Bravo! Luc, quelle est l'activité préférée de Jean?*

Luc : *Jean aime _____.*

Enseignant(e) : *Très bien. Luc, pose la question à Nicole.*

Model Language
- *Quelle est l'activité préférée de _____?*
- *Il aime _____.*
- *Elle aime _____.*

---

2. Anchor Chart (*Tableau de références*)

An Anchor Chart serves as a visual reference for students. It may be posted on a classroom wall or displayed on a flip chart. Anchor Charts include…

- useful classroom expressions;

- sentence starters and models;

- steps to use comprehension strategies, etc.

Example: Anchor Charts for Comprehension Strategies

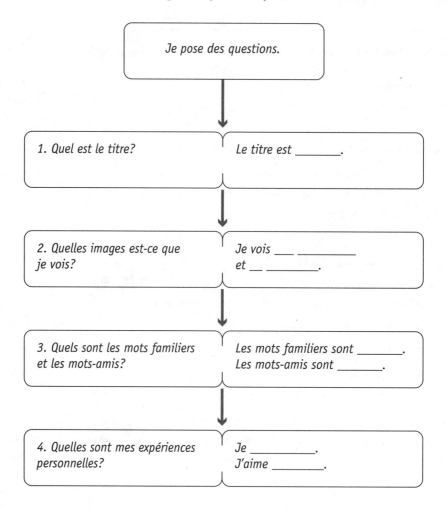

Stratégie : Je pose des questions

Je pose des questions.

1. Quel est le titre? — Le titre est _____.

2. Quelles images est-ce que je vois? — Je vois ___ _____ et __ _____.

3. Quels sont les mots familiers et les mots-amis? — Les mots familiers sont _____. Les mots-amis sont _____.

4. Quelles sont mes expériences personnelles? — Je _____. J'aime _____.

3. Anticipation Guide (*Guide d'anticipation*)

An Anticipation Guide is used to access prior knowledge and provides a structure for making predictions and finding information. Teachers give students a series of statements related to the text and ask them to guess or state their opinion, and then confirm or compare their responses *after* exploring the text. This allows students to check how new information has enhanced their knowledge. They may make and verify their predictions or opinions with peers before and/or after exploring a text.

Example: *Les festivals au Canada*

A. Avant de regarder le film, je lis les descriptions. Je coche (☑) vrai ou faux.

B. Je regarde le film et je relis les descriptions. Je coche (☑) vrai ou faux.

	Avant		Après	
	Vrai	**Faux**	**Vrai**	**Faux**
1. *Chaque province a un festival spécial.*	❑	❑	❑	❑
2. *Tous les festivals sont semblables.*	❑	❑	❑	❑
3. *Tous les festivals sont différents.*	❑	❑	❑	❑

4. Assessment for Learning Tools
(Outils d'évaluation des apprentissages)

Assessment *for* Learning can have a strong, positive impact on student learning, motivation, and self-confidence. Teachers assess to support learning and offer descriptive feedback to coach and help the learner.

There are various types of assessment tools that teachers use to collect and organize information. These tools help teachers to…

- collect evidence;

- plan, differentiate, and improve instruction;

- monitor how well students are learning;

- identify students who are having difficulty in order to provide additional scaffolding and support;

- provide students with descriptive feedback;

- provide evidence for evaluation and reporting purposes.

Example A
Observations: *Les activités orales*

Teachers may use observation checklists for ongoing assessment during all phases of a learning sequence. The criteria included in a checklist may vary depending on the learning outcomes of the task or learning sequence.

Barème : *1 = Rarement / À développer* *2 = Parfois / Satisfaisant* *3 = Souvent / Bien* *4 = Toujours / Très bien* **Nom de l'élève**	*Parle assez fort et clairement.*	*Fait un effort pour parler français.*	*Utilise une aide-visuelle.*			
1.						
2.						
3.						
4.						
5.						

Example B
Shared Assessment: *Évaluation des apprentissages*

Shared assessment may be completed by students and teachers on an
ongoing basis during a learning sequence, and may be shared with parents.

Barème : 1 = Rarement / À développer 2 = Parfois / Satisfaisant 3 = Souvent / Bien 4 = Toujours / Très bien	Moi	Mon enseignant / Mon enseignante	Commentaires
Avant **a)** J'identifie les mots familiers et les mots-amis.	1 2 3 4	1 2 3 4	
b) Je fais des prédictions.	1 2 3 4	1 2 3 4	
Pendant **c)** J'identifie l'idée principale.	1 2 3 4	1 2 3 4	
d) Je compare.	1 2 3 4	1 2 3 4	
Après **e)** Je pose des questions à un ou une partenaire.	1 2 3 4	1 2 3 4	
f) J'écris un message.	1 2 3 4	1 2 3 4	
g) Je présente mon travail.	1 2 3 4	1 2 3 4	
Les commentaires de mes parents :			

Example C
Self-assessment / Reflection: *Auto-évaluation / Réflexion*

Self-assessment / Reflection allows students to take responsibility of their own learning. Teachers should vary their approach from lesson to lesson, and focus students' reflection by linking it to the most recent learning they have done.

Individual self-assessment/reflection: Teachers may use a grid to help students reflect on their level of participation or suggest questions to reflect on a strategy used in a particular lesson sequence.

Class reflection: From time to time, at the end of a class period, a week, or a learning sequence, the teacher may conduct an oral class reflection. Students are asked to recall activities, new words and expressions, and cultural information, and record their responses in an idea web.

Individual Reflection on a Strategy

Avant

1. *J'utilise la stratégie :* <u>*Je fais des prédictions.*</u>

2. *Ma prédiction est* _____ .

   a) *Le titre est* _____ .

   b) *Je vois* _____ .

   c) *Les mots familiers et les mots-amis sont :*

     _____   _____

     _____   _____

     _____   _____

Après

3. *Ma prédiction…* ☐ *est juste.*

                 ☐ *n'est pas juste.*

4. *Cette stratégie m'aide…*

pas du tout	*un peu*	*assez*	*beaucoup*

---

5. Checklist for Choosing Texts
(*Liste de contrôle pour choisir des textes*)

Choosing the right text is central to motivating and engaging students.
Teachers may evaluate texts using criteria related to students' level of
readability, language level, and level of interest.

Example: Choosing and Assessing Text

Ideal Characteristics	Usually	Somewhat	Rarely
• The language is accurate, simple, direct, concise (few needless words).			
• The language maintains a consistent level throughout the entire text.			
• The visuals are rich, attractive, abundant, and clearly convey meaning.			
• The text is long enough to tell a story or from which to gather information but short enough to be accessible and sustain interest.			
• The text uses authentic language and provides good examples of real discourse in French.			
• The text contains language and information that are at appropriate cognitive and language levels.			
• The text includes themes, situations, and characters that represent students' interests, experiences, and cultural/linguistic backgrounds.			
• The text follows a logical sequence. For example, a narrative text includes a clear beginning, middle, and end. In a biography, the text is presented chronologically.			
• An aural or audiovisual text contains meaningful sound effects, one or two different voices and clear, slow speech (yet not so slow that it seems artificial to students).			
• An aural or audiovisual text represents a variety of voices including male and female voices, native Francophones, and learners of French.			

6. Coding a Text (*Encodage d'un texte*)

Teachers may encourage students to code a text, that is, listen to, view, or read a text again with a specific purpose and mark certain elements. An aural or visual text may be coded on a chart using sticky notes, while a written text may be coded using a highlighter. Coding can be used as a means of identifying personal connections to a text or to increase language awareness. Once students have coded a text, they may share their results with a partner or use them for details in a follow-up piece of writing. In FSL, teachers should ensure that students have used the language before they code the text. Teachers should present and display language models to be used by students in coding the text before the task.

Example: Familiar Words and Cognates

Model Language

Je note les mots familiers. _Bonjour_ *est un mot familier.*

J'identifie les mots-amis. _Le hockey_ *est un mot-ami.*

a)

Bonjour! Ici Tyler. Ma famille habite à Windsor en Nouvelle-Écosse. Je parle français et anglais. La nature est très belle dans les provinces maritimes. J'adore les pommes.

b)

Salut! Je m'appelle Lilyanne. J'habite à Canmore en Alberta. Je parle polonais et anglais, et j'apprends le français aussi. J'adore la randonnée dans les montagnes!

c)

Salut! Ici, Tomas. J'ai 9 ans. Ma famille habite à Old Crow au Yukon. Je parle tutchone, tchèque et anglais et j'apprends le français. Voici l'aurore boréale. C'est beau, n'est-ce pas ?

7. Draw What I Say (*Écoutez et dessinez*)

Draw What I Say may be used in FSL classrooms as a vocabulary reinforcement game or an assessment tool. The teacher (or a student) reads a description of a scene and the listeners draw the scene according to the description. Then, students could be asked to retell what they heard by describing what they have drawn, or they may use the description as a clue to answer a question. For example, in a learning sequence on clothing, students could be asked to listen to descriptions of young people wearing various clothing items, draw what they hear, and then guess the season.

Example: *Devinette*

Model Language

- *Dessinez le garçon.*

- *Il porte un pantalon court noir et un t-shirt rouge.*

  Il porte des souliers de sport. Il joue au soccer.

- *Voici une devinette : C'est quelle saison?*

C'est le printemps!

8. Fish Bone (*Diagramme cause-effet*)

A Fish Bone graphic organizer is used to sort information. In FSL, the Fish Bone organizer may be used for a narrative or informative text. The Fish Bone organizer may be used to identify and organize words and ideas in the text. The topic is written in the head of the fish, the main ideas are written into the spine of the fish, and the supporting details are added to the fish bones.

Example: *Des insectes*

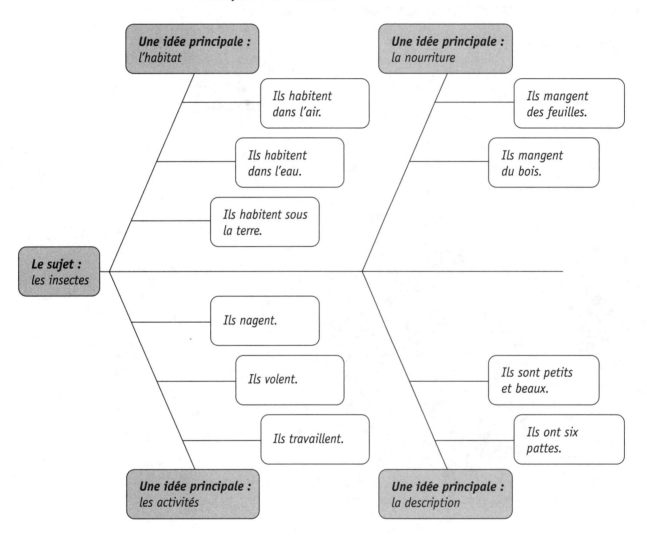

9. Flow Chart (*Organigramme*)

A Flow Chart is a graphic presentation or diagram using symbols to show the step-by-step sequence or progression of events. The order is determined by decisions or outcomes at each step. Students may use a Flow Chart to understand the events of a story. They may also use a Flow Chart to outline the steps to take when using a strategy. For example, students may use a Flow Chart to monitor and verify their understanding of a listening selection.

Example: *Les collations*

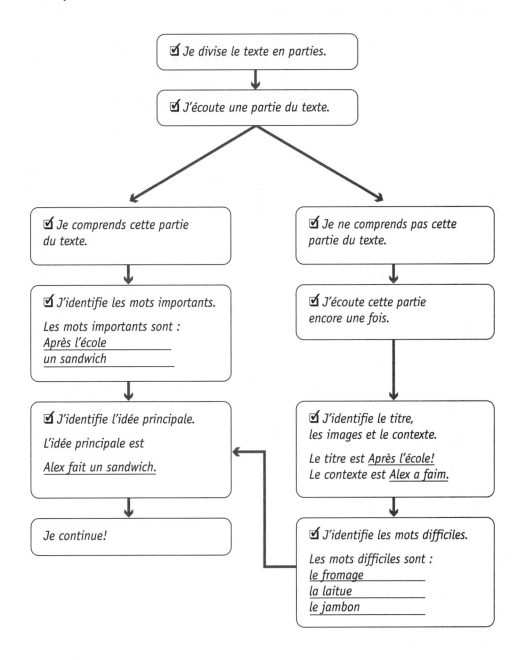

10. Inquiry Chart (*Tableau d'enquête*)

The benefit of an Inquiry Chart is to help students organize and summarize key information during and/or after exploring a text. At the beginning, an Inquiry Chart can be completed as a whole class. Once students are comfortable with using the chart, and with the types of questions that are asked, they may complete a chart either with a partner or independently. To add challenge to an Inquiry Chart, students may add observations gleaned from the text.

Example: *Les festivals au Canada*

	Le Stampede de Calgary	*Le Festival du voyageur*
Où? **Où est le festival?**	*Le Stampede est à Calgary en Alberta.*	*Le Festival du voyageur est* ____ _____ _____ _____.
Quand? **Quelle est la date?**	*C'est en juillet.*	*C'est* _____ _____.
Quoi? **Quelles sont les activités?**	*Il y a un rodéo.* *Il y a un défilé.*	*Il y a* _____ _____.

11. Interview (*Entrevue*)

After students have explored a narrative text, they may role-play an Interview with one of the characters in the text. To begin, the teacher and students brainstorm a list of questions. Next, they work on an Interview together. Finally, students create their own Interview by adapting the model that they worked on together. They may alternate playing the character and/or the reporter with a partner. To add challenge, students may add their own questions to the Interview.

Example: Spider-Man

Model Language

Élève 1 (Journaliste) : *Bonjour! Comment t'appelles-tu?*

Élève 2 (Spider-Man) : <u>*Moi, je m'appelle Spider-Man!*</u>

Élève 1 (Journaliste) : *Eh bien… tu es célèbre. Pourquoi?*

Élève 2 (Spider-Man) : <u>*Je suis un superhéros.*</u>

Élève 1 (Journaliste) : *Comment es-tu?*

Élève 2 (Spider-Man) : <u>*Je suis courageux et fort.*</u>

Élève 1 (Journaliste) : *Merci!*

12. K-W-L and K-W-L Plus Charts
(*Tableaux SVA et SVA Plus*)

A K-W-L (Know/Want to Know/Learned) Chart (i.e., *un Tableau SVA*) is a graphic organizer that activates students' prior knowledge, stimulates inquiry about the topic, and identifies newly acquired information. The K-W-L Chart is used in the *before, during,* and *after* components of exploring a text.

At the beginning, the K-W-L Chart can be completed as a whole class. Once students are comfortable using the K-W-L Chart, they can complete it either with a partner or independently.

The *Plus* column can be added to the K-W-L Chart as a further challenge. It encourages students to make observations about the information learned in the text.

Example: *Une affiche qui annonce un concert de musique*

A. AVANT l'exploration du texte...

- *Je note mes connaissances (S).*
- *Je pose des questions (V).*

B. APRÈS l'exploration du texte...

- *Je réponds aux questions (A).*
- *Je fais des observations (+).*

S *Qu'est-ce que je sais?*	V *Qu'est-ce que je veux savoir?*	A *Qu'est-ce que j'apprends?*	+ *Je fais des observations.*
• On annonce un concert. • J'adore les concerts de musique.	• Quelle sorte de musique est-ce? • Qui est l'artiste? • Quelle est la date du concert? • Où est le concert?	• C'est de la musique rock. • C'est Justin Timberlake. • C'est le 22 août. • C'est à Moncton au Nouveau-Brunswick.	• Le concert est dehors.

13. Language Games (*Jeux*)

Language Games enhance class dynamics and increase language learning enjoyment. Games that are used effectively have a communicative goal. To develop fluency in French, students are encouraged to use complete sentences while playing games.

Example A: *La chaîne des activités*

To facilitate learning how to describe personal and peer preference using *aimer*, the teacher may introduce the game *La chaîne des activités* similar to the well-known game *Je fais ma valise*. To begin the game, a student identifies his or her favourite activity in a complete sentence. The next student turns to the previous one, identifies who he or she is referring to, recalls what all previous students have said, and adds his or her own favourite activity. The game continues until the chain is broken or when all the students have participated.

Model Language

Élève 1 : *J'aime la bicyclette.*

Élève 2 : *Tu aimes la bicyclette. J'aime les jeux vidéo.*

Élève 3 : *Elle aime la bicyclette. Tu aimes les jeux vidéo. J'adore le soccer.*

Élève 4 : *Elle aime la bicyclette. Il aime les jeux vidéo. Tu adores le soccer. J'aime le volleyball.*

Example B: *La chaîne des questions et des réponses*

The following game is another example of a chain activity and may be used to reinforce listening skills. To begin, the teacher prepares a series of questions and answers that relate to a particular topic, and writes the questions and answers on index cards that are distributed to students. One student reads his/her question while the other students must read their cards to determine if they have the answer. The student with the appropriate answer reads it aloud and then turns his/her card over and reads the next question.

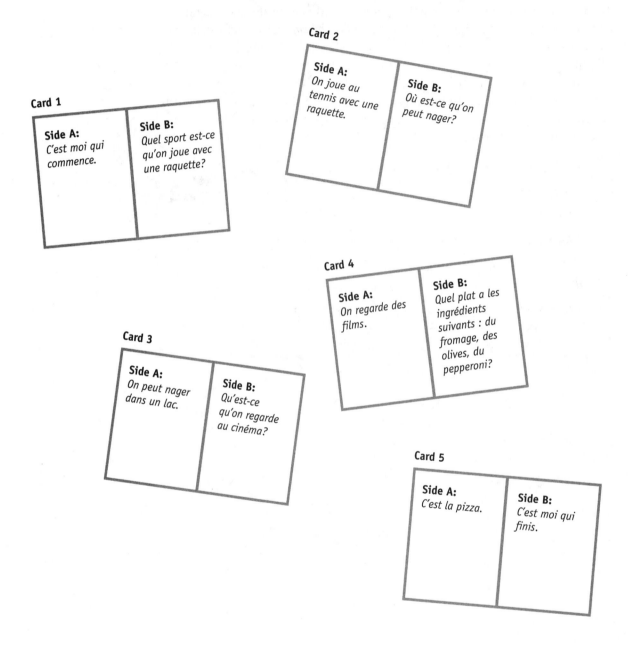

Card 1

Side A: *C'est moi qui commence.*

Side B: *Quel sport est-ce qu'on joue avec une raquette?*

Card 2

Side A: *On joue au tennis avec une raquette.*

Side B: *Où est-ce qu'on peut nager?*

Card 3

Side A: *On peut nager dans un lac.*

Side B: *Qu'est-ce qu'on regarde au cinéma?*

Card 4

Side A: *On regarde des films.*

Side B: *Quel plat a les ingrédients suivants : du fromage, des olives, du pepperoni?*

Card 5

Side A: *C'est la pizza.*

Side B: *C'est moi qui finis.*

14. Learning Log/Journal (*Journal de bord*)

A Learning Log or Journal is an excellent way for students to personalize and demonstrate their learning. At a beginning level, students may create an illustration and add simple captions for an entry in their Learning Log. Later, they may be able to write simple sentences. The information gathered from a Learning Log/Journal enables teachers to monitor student learning over time, provide students with descriptive feedback, and identify those who are having difficulty in order to provide additional scaffolding and support.

Example: *Les messages*

Leçon 1 : Je lis six messages.

1. *Mon message préféré est le message de* ___Tyler___ .

2. *Voici des mots familiers et des mots-amis :* ___français___ ,
   ___la nature___ ,
   ___les provinces maritimes___ ,
   ___les pommes___ .

Leçon 2 : Je réponds à des questions personnelles.

1. *Je m'appelle* ___Max___ .

2. *J'habite* ___à Camrose, en Alberta___ .

3. *Je parle* ___anglais___ , ___ukrainien___ *et j'apprends le* ___français___ .

4. *Quelle activité est-ce que tu aimes? J'aime* ___faire de la bicyclette___ .

Leçon 3 : Je compare.

1. *Qui est semblable à moi? C'est* ___Jacob___ .

2. *Explique...* ___Jacob___ *aime* ___le hockey___ *et moi aussi!*

3. *Qui n'est pas comme moi? C'est* ___Tanya___ .

4. *Explique...* ___Tanya___ *aime* ___faire de la natation___
   mais moi, j'aime ___écouter de la musique___ .

Leçon 4 : Je réfléchis.

1. *C'est facile pour moi :* _____

2. *C'est difficile pour moi :* _____

3. *J'aime* _____ .

4. *J'ai besoin de pratiquer :* _____

---

15. Numbered Heads (*Têtes numérotées*)

Numbered Heads is a strategy that requires students to be individually accountable. It is often used in the context of group work. Each student is assigned a number or a letter. When selecting students to respond to questions or perform certain tasks in the class, the teacher randomly chooses a number or a letter. All the students with that number or letter will respond to the question individually.

Example: *Les messages*

Model Language

Enseignant(e) *: Qui aime les pommes? Hmm… Les numéros 2, s'il vous plaît… Oui, Marco?*

Marco *: C'est Gabriel. Il aime les pommes.*

Enseignant(e) *: Très bien! Maintenant, où est-ce que Gabriel habite? Les numéros 4, s'il vous plaît… Oui, Sélina?*

Sélina *: Gabriel habite en Nouvelle-Écosse.*

Enseignant(e) *: Excellent!*

---

16. Place Mat (*Napperon*)

A Place Mat organizer is a cooperative activity in which a small group of students (two to four students) provides information about a text. The group then writes a common answer in the middle square.

To create a Place Mat organizer, divide a large sheet of paper or Place Mat into equal sections. Each student completes his or her section of the Place Mat, either with illustrations or written text. Next, the Place Mat is rotated to the right (or left) and students read each of the group members' responses one at a time. Finally, the group decides on its common answers and writes them in the centre of the Place Mat.

Example: *Nos passe-temps*

In the following example, the teacher begins by brainstorming a list of pastimes with the whole class. The teacher then models her three favourite pastimes. Students adapt the model and write three things they like to do in their spare time in their section of the Place Mat.

> **Model Language**
>
> *Comme passe-temps, j'aime* _____.

A. *J'écris mes passe-temps préférés.*

B. *Ensuite, nous comparons nos passe-temps.*

C. *Finalement, nous écrivons nos passe-temps en commun dans le centre.*

Mon nom : <u>Ahmed</u>
Comme passe-temps…
J'aime collectionner les cartes de hockey.
J'adore écouter de la musique.

Mon nom : <u>Samantha</u>
Comme passe-temps…
J'adore jouer au soccer.
J'adore les concerts de musique.

> ***Notre groupe aime la musique.***
> * *Ahmed adore écouter de la musique.*
> * *Samantha adore les concerts de musique.*
> * *Kevin aime jouer de la guitare.*
> * *Marissa adore chanter.*

Mon nom : <u>Kevin</u>
Comme passe-temps…
J'aime jouer de la guitare.
Aussi, j'adore faire du camping.

Mon nom : <u>Marissa</u>
Comme passe-temps…
J'aime faire de la planche à roulettes.
J'adore chanter.

---

17. Plus-Minus-Interesting Chart
(*Tableau plus / moins / intéressant*)

The Plus-Minus-Interesting Chart encourages students to compare, synthesize, and analyse information. Plus refers to a positive aspect; Minus refers to a negative aspect; and Interesting refers to personal observations or decisions made after weighing the positive and negative aspects.

It is a good idea to create positive and negative statements with students by making observations or decisions as a class. Alternatively, teachers may provide choices for individual reflection.

For example, after exploring a text about playing soccer, the teacher and students create a Plus-Minus-Interesting Chart using information found in text.

Example: *Le soccer*

A. *Je note les aspects positifs et les aspects négatifs dans la bonne colonne.*

B. *Ensuite, je note ma décision.*

+	–	*Intéressant*
Voici des aspects positifs... • *On est très actif. C'est bon pour la santé.* • *C'est un jeu coopératif.*	*Voici des aspects négatifs...* • *C'est un peu dangereux.* • *C'est un sport fatigant.*	*Voici ma décision...* • *Je veux jouer au soccer.* *ou* • *Je ne veux pas jouer au soccer.*

18. Portfolio (*Portfolio*)

A Portfolio gives students and teachers the opportunity to collect exemplars of student learning to be kept in a personal folder. This collection tells the story of the student's efforts, progress, and achievement in a given learning sequence. Throughout the year, teachers and students may select specific pieces that demonstrate their learning and are representative of their progress.

Example A: Suggested list of Portfolio items for a learning sequence on e-mail messages

> *Mon portfolio*
> - *Une opinion : mon message préféré*
> - *Un diagramme de Venn*
> - *Une activité d'écoute : des messages*
> - *Un dessin : mon activité préférée*
> - *Mon message*
> - *Mon auto-évaluation*
> - *Une évaluation par mon enseignant(e)*

Example B: Self-assessment Form

La date :

A. Le titre de mon travail est _____.

B. Ce travail...

☐ *est bien fait. J'ai fait un effort. J'aime _____ _____.*

☐ *est assez bien fait. Je veux changer _____ _____.*

☐ *n'est pas très bien. La prochaine fois, je _____ _____.*

19. Retelling and Role Play (*Narration et jeu de rôles*)

After exploring a text, students may benefit by using various activities that provide further opportunities for them to develop oral language and make connections between the text and themselves. Students use Retelling and Role Play to transform information in the text into a new form in various ways.

1. **Matching Activity:** Students retell a story by matching a series of images and corresponding sentences relating to the text and by sequencing them in a logical order. Subsequently, they may read their version of the story aloud to a partner.

2. **Sentence Strips:** Students arrange a series of sentence strips relating to the text. They then retell their story orally to a partner.

3. **Role Play:** Students may take the oral reading one step further by transforming the story into a role play.

Example: Sentence Strips

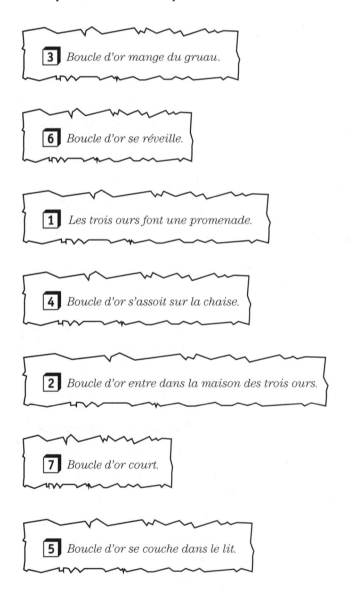

3 *Boucle d'or mange du gruau.*

6 *Boucle d'or se réveille.*

1 *Les trois ours font une promenade.*

4 *Boucle d'or s'assoit sur la chaise.*

2 *Boucle d'or entre dans la maison des trois ours.*

7 *Boucle d'or court.*

5 *Boucle d'or se couche dans le lit.*

20. Sentence Starters and Models
(*Débuts de phrase et modèles*)

Sentence Starters and Models are an effective way to help students use the language authentically. Teachers scaffold the learning in order to gradually release responsibility to the students by providing models, and supporting them through shared and guided practice as they adapt the models until they can use the language independently.

Example: Sentence Starters

– *Je m'appelle* _____.

– *J'habite à* _____ _____.

– *Je parle* _____ *et* _____.

– *J'aime* _____.

Example: Models

– *Je m'appelle Lucie.*

– *J'habite à Régina en Saskatchewan.*

– *Je parle anglais et français.*

– *J'aime jouer de la guitare.*

21. Story Map (*Schéma du récit*)

Story Mapping is a technique used after a narrative text has been listened to, viewed, or read to visually represent the key elements and events, and to show the connections among ideas. To begin, the teacher and students identify the setting, main characters, and story problem. Next, they describe the sequence of the events in the text. After the Story Map is complete, students may use it to retell the story, illustrate the main events, or act it out.

Example: *Boucles d'or et les trois ours*

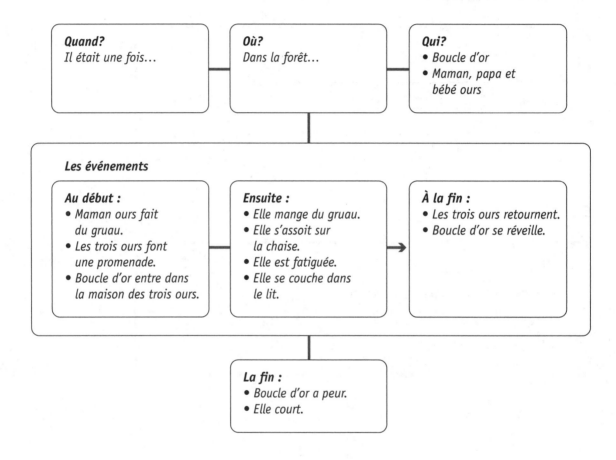

22. Timeline (*Ligne de temps*)

A Timeline is a type of graphic organizer that is useful in summarizing informative text or biographies. The events of the text are organized chronologically.

Example
Terry Fox : Une ligne de temps

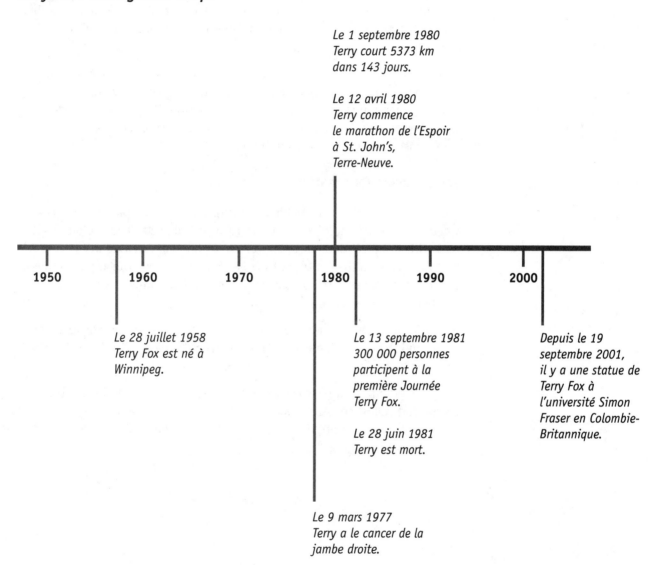

Le 1 septembre 1980
Terry court 5373 km
dans 143 jours.

Le 12 avril 1980
Terry commence
le marathon de l'Espoir
à St. John's,
Terre-Neuve.

1950 1960 1970 1980 1990 2000

Le 28 juillet 1958
Terry Fox est né à
Winnipeg.

Le 13 septembre 1981
300 000 personnes
participent à la
première Journée
Terry Fox.

Le 28 juin 1981
Terry est mort.

Depuis le 19
septembre 2001,
il y a une statue de
Terry Fox à
l'université Simon
Fraser en Colombie-
Britannique.

Le 9 mars 1977
Terry a le cancer de la
jambe droite.

23. Traffic Light (*Signalisation*)

The Traffic Light is a visual tool that students may place on their desks to demonstrate their level of understanding during a lesson. Students use this visual, which could be a three-colour disk for example, to indicate that they fully understand (by pointing to the green light); that they understand partially but they require more support (by pointing to the amber light); or that they do not understand and require additional instruction and support (by pointing to the red light). In this way, students are able to self-assess their own learning, and teachers can monitor their understanding and adjust instruction during a lesson sequence.

Alternatively, students can indicate their level of comprehension at certain points in a lesson by placing their fist (do not understand), two fingers (partially understand) or open hand (fully understand) against their chest. The teacher can say *Montrez-moi si vous comprenez* and quickly get a general sense of students' understanding.

Example: Ideas for Creating a Traffic Light

1. **Circular disks:** Students begin by cutting a disk out of paper or light-weight cardboard and dividing it into three equal parts. They colour each part with a different colour using yellow, green, and red, and insert a movable arrow in the centre of the disk. Students move the arrow to the appropriate colour to reflect their level of understanding during a lesson sequence.

2. **Recycle old CDs:** Students cover one side of a CD with red construction paper and the other side with green construction paper. Students display the side of the CD that reflects their level of comprehension.

3. **Flags:** Students create two or three flags using Popsicle sticks and red, green, and yellow construction paper. They display the appropriate flag or position the appropriate flag in a cup holder on their desk to reflect their level of understanding.

24. Venn Diagram (*Diagramme de Venn*)

A Venn Diagram is a graphic organizer that students use to compare and contrast ideas or items and to identify common elements. The characteristics of each item are listed in each section of the diagram, and the shared characteristics are listed in the overlapping section.

Example: *Je compare les collations préférées dans la classe.*

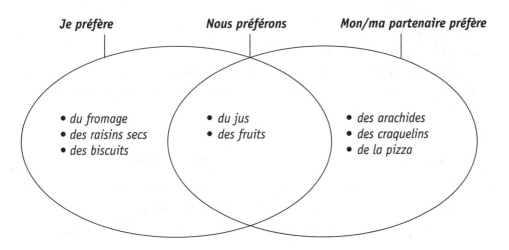

Je préfère
- du fromage
- des raisins secs
- des biscuits

Nous préférons
- du jus
- des fruits

Mon/ma partenaire préfère
- des arachides
- des craquelins
- de la pizza

25. Word Sorts (*Triages de mots*)

Word Sorts are activities that require students to group together words or images according to specific criteria. Words may be grouped according to a sound and/or symbol relationship, familiar words and cognates, or word families. Alternatively, a Word Sort may require students to identify a word that is different than the others in a particular set. Words or images may also be provided on flash cards or slips of paper and given to students in an envelope for sorting.

Example A
Les collations : le son «g»

For example, in a lesson sequence on food, students could be asked to cut out the following words and group together words that have a soft "g" and a hard "g" sound.

une boisson gazeuse	*un yogourt*
une orange	*de la crème glacée*
une barre granola	*du fromage*
un tangerine	*un ingrédient*

Example B
La musique : Quel mot est différent?

				Le son semblable
1. *Cette musique est...*	*calmante*	*irritante*	*énergique*	*ante*
2. *Cette musique est...*	*passionnante*	*rythmée*	*intéressante*	*ante*
3. *Le CD est...*	*mémorable*	*remarquable*	*captivant*	
4. *Le CD est...*	*romantique*	*bon*	*énergique*	
5. *Cette chanson est...*	*expressive*	*branchée*	*rythmée*	

26. Word Wall/Vocabulary Bank
(*Mur de mots / Banque de vocabulaire*)

A Word Wall or Vocabulary Bank is a display or grouping of theme-related or topic-related words that serves as a reference for students. It provides a means of scaffolding vocabulary and organizing words according to patterns. Words may be categorized in various ways and for different purposes. For example, they may be organized by subtopic, cognates, familiar words, or sound-and-symbol relationships.

The development of a Word Wall/Vocabulary Bank is ongoing and will change for every learning sequence. Word choices for the Word Wall/Vocabulary Bank are chosen from texts and from the students' own experiences. Word choices are written with an article or in complete sentences, e.g., *les devoirs* or *Je fais les devoirs*.

Example: Ideas for Creating a Word Wall/Vocabulary Bank

1. **Word Wall:** A bulletin board, wall, or blackboard area may be designated where words or simple phrases may be added individually using construction paper and a temporary adhesive to allow for the organizing and reorganizing of words to suit a particular task.

2. **Chart Paper:** Vocabulary lists may be displayed on chart paper when a language classroom is not available. In conjunction with these charts, vocabulary words on slips of paper may be provided for easy manipulation by students.

3. **Illustrated Idea Web:** Words can be organized in a word web and students can illustrate the web to create a visual reference.

4. **Personal Dictionaries:** Students may create their own personal illustrated Vocabulary Bank.

27. Word Web (*Toile de mots*)

A Word Web is a tool used to record the results of a brainstorming session. Word Webs may be displayed for easy reference, for example, on chart paper, on an overhead transparency, on a whiteboard, or on a computer using Kidspiration™ or a similar program. The topic is written in the centre of the web and students are invited to complete it with previously-learned as well as new vocabulary.

Example: *Les collations*

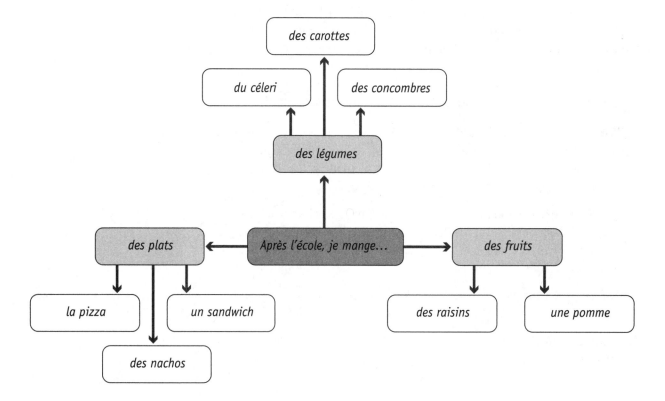

effective literacy practices in **FSL: making connections**

Appendix B:
Glossary

Légende
exp.   *expression*
loc.   *locution*
n.m.   *nom masculin*
n.f.   *nom féminin*
v.   *verbe*
pl.   *pluriel*

AB Partnering (*Travail en partenaires, n.m.*) : Tactic whereby students are responsible for reporting their partner's information to the class.

action research (*recherche-action, n.f.*) : The gathering and analysis of data by educators for the purpose of refining instruction.

active/passive vocabulary (*langage expressif / réceptif, n.m.*) : Students' active vocabulary is comprised of words they know and use while their passive vocabulary includes words to which they can respond appropriately but have not incorporated into their own vocabulary.

activity centres (*centres d'apprentissage, n.m.pl.*) : Work stations in a classroom that provide independent listening, viewing, reading, art, or computer activities.

additional language (*langue additionnelle, n.f.*) : A language other than English spoken by the student.

Anchor Chart (*Tableau de références, n.m.*) : Chart designed by the teacher or class that lists procedures, or serves as a memory aid.

anticipation (*anticipation, n.f.*) : A step in the instructional sequence in which students identify what they might expect to find before they listen to, view, or read a text.

Anticipation Guide (*Guide d'anticipation, n.m.*) : A set of questions that guides student predictions before and after listening to, viewing, or reading a text.

Assessment *for* Learning (*Outils d'évaluation des apprentissages, n.f.*) : Ongoing processes that the teacher uses, formally and informally, to monitor student progress with authentic tasks, adjust teaching based on this information, and involve students in their own learning.

Assessment *of* Learning (*Évaluation sommative, n.f.*) : Judgement determined by the teacher about student learning at a certain point in time.

assessment tools (*outils d'évaluation, n.m.pl.*) : Various ways of gathering assessment information from students including observation sheets, checklists, and rubrics.

authentic task (*tâche authentique, n.f.*) : A project that is of interest to students and relates to their real-life experiences.

authentic text (*texte authentique, n.m.*) : Aural, audiovisual, electronic, graphic, or written texts that are of interest to students and relate to their real-life experiences.

big book and small book (*livre grand format et petit format, n.m.*) : Big books are large format books used in shared reading while small books can be read by students to their peers, to younger children, or independently.

bilingual text (*texte bilingue, n.m.*) : Texts that appear in two languages and used in second language settings to validate students' first language.

Bloom's taxonomy (*taxonomie de Bloom, n.f.*) : An instructional organizer developed by B. Bloom providing questions categorized by level of difficulty used in the classroom to elicit varying levels of thinking skills.

book rap (*discussion par courriel, n.f.*) : Online e-mail discussions conducted by individuals or groups of students.

brainstorming (*remue-méninges, n.m.*) : A tactic that invites students to volunteer ideas for a topic in which all ideas are accepted without judgement.

breaking the code (*décodage, n.m.*) : Skills and knowledge about language forms and language awareness used to make sense of aural, visual, and written text.

Checklist for Choosing Text (*Liste de contrôle pour choisir des textes, n.f.*) : Checklist for evaluating texts using criteria related to readability, language level, and level of interest.

choral reading (*lecture en chœur, n.f.*) : An interpretive reading of a text by students, individually, in pairs, or in unison.

code-breaker (*décodeur / encodeur, n.m.*) : One of the four roles of the literate student. The student uses language forms and language awareness to make sense of text.

Coding a Text (*Encodage d'un texte, n.m.*) : A physical means used to "mark" the text in order to add personal commentary.

cognates (*mots-amis, n.m.pl.*) : Words that have a similar or identical form in two or more languages.

cognitive processes (*processus cognitifs, n.m.pl.*) : Ways in which the brain processes information and students learn.

cognitively challenging text (*texte ayant un défi cognitif, n.m.*) : Text that stimulates the student's cognitive processes.

communicative task (*tâche communicative, n.f.*) : Work that allows students to communicate for a real purpose.

communicative-experiential approach (*approche communicative-expérientielle, n.f.*) : A framework whereby students work on projects or tasks that allow them to use language to communicate for a real purpose and to perform real-life tasks.

context clues (*indices contextuels, n.m.pl.*) : Use of information within a text to make meaning.

contextualization (*contextualisation, n.f.*) : A step in the instructional sequence in which students are introduced to a topic before the text is listened to, viewed, or read.

continuum (*continuum, n.m.*) : A gradual transition in a student's learning from one state to another without abrupt changes.

critical literacy skills (*habiletés en lecture critique, n.f.pl.*) : A process of looking beyond the literal meaning of texts to determine the author's intent, and the beliefs and values that are conveyed in the text.

culturally-relevant text (*texte ayant un sens culturel, n.m.*) : Text that examines culture in its broad sense and reflects the potential diversity of student life experiences.

decode (*décoder, v.*) : Understand text by identifying patterns.

differentiated instruction (*enseignement différencié, n.m.*) : Teaching that meets the wide range of learning needs within a classroom using pre-planned and mid-course interventions.

discourse (*discours, n.m.*) : Text with a specific purpose.

Draw What I Say (*Écoutez et dessinez, loc.*) : Tactic used to help students visualize or to assess their level of understanding.

Dual-iceberg Theory (*Théorie de l'iceberg, n.f.*) : Theory developed by J. Cummins whereby first-language proficiencies can be transferred to second-language learning, and vice versa.

elementary FSL students (*élèves en FLS au deuxième cycle du primaire, n.m.pl.*) : Grades 4–8 students in most Canadian provinces.

engagement (*engagement, n.m.*) : Student commitment to learning French; engagement is not a synonym for participation.

enunciation (*articulation, n.f.*) : To articulate sounds.

evaluation (*évaluation sommative, n.f.*) : See "assessment *of* learning."

familiar words (*mots familiers, n.m.pl.*) : Words that students already know that do not pose a barrier to understanding text.

faux-amis (*faux-amis, n.m.pl.*) : An English and French word that looks the same in both languages but has a different meaning. e.g., sensible and *sensible.*

Fish Bone (*Diagramme cause-effet, n.m.*) : A graphic organizer used to sort information. The topic is written in the "head" of the fish, the main ideas on the spine, and the supporting details are added to the fish bones.

Flow Chart (*organigramme, n.m.*) : A graphic organizer that shows a sequence or progression of steps, in which the order is determined by decisions or outcomes at each step.

fluency (*aisance, n.f.*) : Student ability to use language easily and accurately.

Gradual Release of Responsibility (*Transfert graduel de responsabilité, n.m.*) : An approach whereby the teacher provides support to help students grow in their knowledge and use of French, then gradually withdraws support as students become more independent in their learning. The four steps are modelling, shared practice, guided practice, and independent practice.

graphic novel (*bande dessinée romanesque, n.f.*) : An illustrated story presented in comic book format.

graphic organizer (*organisateur graphique, n.m.*) : A chart that enables students to visually represent information, relationships between ideas, and their own thoughts on a subject.

graphophonics (*graphophonétique, n.f.*) : Relationship between symbols (the letters of the alphabet) and the sounds they make when pronounced.

groupings (*groupes, n.m.pl.*) : Groups of students within a classroom may be skill-based or interest-based, heterogeneous or homogeneous, purposeful or random.

guided practice (*pratique guidée, n.f.*) : The third of four incremental steps in the gradual release of responsibility model. The teacher provides support and guidance as students complete a task.

independent practice (*pratique autonome, n.f.*) : The last of four incremental steps in the gradual release of responsibility model. Students are ready to accomplish a task on their own.

input hypothesis (*hypothèse de l'exposition à la langue cible, n.f.*) : Hypothesis developed by Krashen that suggests second language acquisition progresses when students receive input that is one step beyond their level of linguistic competence.

Inquiry Chart (*Tableau d'enquête, n.m.*) : A graphic organizer used to explore a subject by asking questions and looking for answers within one or more texts.

instructional tactics (*tactiques d'enseignement, n.f.pl.*) : Actions initiated by the teacher to organize student involvement in a specific activity.

interview (*entrevue, n.f.*) : A tactic whereby students adapt and personalize a model interview.

intonation (*intonation, n.f.*) : The rise and fall in pitch of the voice in speech.

just-in-time (*juste-à-temps, loc.*) : An instructional concept promoting the idea that language patterns be taught in context as students need them to understand or communicate.

K-W-L and K-W-L Plus Chart (*Tableau SVA et Tableau SVA Plus, n.m.*) : A graphic organizer that activates students' background knowledge, stimulates inquiry about the topic, and identifies newly acquired information. **K-W-L:** What I KNOW, what I WANT to know, what I LEARNED. ***Tableau SVA****: Ce que je SAIS, ce que je VEUX savoir, ce que j'ai APPRIS.*

language awareness (*prise de conscience langagière, n.f.*) : Students' capacity to understand how language forms operate and how meaning is made.

language forms (*formes langagières, n.f.pl.*) : Language components, such as grammar, phonics, sentence structure, and spelling patterns.

Learning Log/Journal (*Journal de bord, n.m.*) : A physical place where students may reflect on and improve their learning.

learning strategies (*stratégies d'apprentissage, n.f.pl.*) : Specific actions or techniques students use to enhance their own learning.

learning styles (*styles d'apprentissage, n.m.pl.*) : Instructional organizer that suggests students perceive and process experience in different preferred ways.

linguistic and strategic competence (*compétences linguistiques et stratégiques, n.f.pl.*) : A student's proficiency in using language and strategies.

literacy (*littératie, n.f.*) : The ability to use language and images in rich and varied forms to read, write, listen, speak, view, represent, and think critically about ideas.

literacy continuum (*continuum de développement en littératie, n.m.*) : A scale of learning complexity, whereby students can move to higher levels as they gain experience and success with various skills and strategies.

literacy environment (*environnement propice au développement de la littératie, n.m.*) : The physical and emotional climate in a classroom that promotes literacy objectives.

literacy practices (*pratiques de littératie, n.f.pl.*) : A range of activities that develop and enhance literacy skills and strategies in students using various means of expression, communication, and lifelong learning.

literacy strategy instruction (*enseignement des stratégies de littératie, n.m.*) : The range of strategies that teachers may use to develop literacy skills in students.

literacy teacher (*enseignant chargé d'enseigner la littératie, n.m.*) : A teacher who uses a range of practices to promote literacy skills and strategies in students.

literate learner (*apprenant mettant en pratique ses connaissances en littératie, n.m.*) : A student who uses literacy skills and strategies to understand text and to communicate.

meaning maker (*créateur de sens, n.m.*) : One of the four roles of the literate student: the student uses strategies to understand text.

metacognition (*métacognition, n.f.*) : Learners become aware of and manage their own learning.

mnemonics (*aide à la mémoire, n.f.*) : a device, formula, or code designed as a memory aid.

mode (*moyen, n.m.*) : A means of communication: listening, speaking, reading, writing, viewing, and representing are modes of learning.

modelling (*modéliser, n.f.*) : The first of four incremental steps in the gradual release of responsibility model: the teacher demonstrates a task for students.

monitor and repair (*vérifier sa compréhension, loc.*) : A comprehension strategy aimed at chunking text, being aware of one's understanding, and going back to review text if understanding is impaired.

motivation (*motivation, n.f.*) : Student desire, need, or willingness to learn French. Motivation is a two-fold issue: intrinsic and extrinsic.

multiliteracies (*multilittératies, n.f.pl.*) : A recognition that students are involved in literacy practices with text of all types using all technologies and in languages other than the school language.

multimodal approach (*approche multimodale, n.f.*) : Using and integrating all modes of learning: listening, speaking, reading, writing, viewing, and representing.

multiple intelligences (*intelligences multiples, n.f.pl.*) : Organizer developed by Howard Gardner identifying eight types of intellience: verbal-linguistic, logico-mathematical, musical, visual-spatial, kinaesthetic, natural, interpersonal, and intrapersonal.

Numbered Heads (*Têtes numérotées, loc.*) : A group activity whereby members are assigned numbers or letters. Teachers call on a number or letter at random, thereby making all group members accountable.

output (*production, n.f.*) : Language produced by the student.

personalization (*personalisation, n.f.*) : A step in the instructional sequence in which students make links between a topic and their personal experience and background knowledge.

Place Mat (*Napperon, n.m.*) : A cooperative activity in which a small group of students individually record information on a graphic organizer, then make a group observation.

Plus-Minus-Interesting Chart (*Tableau plus / moins / intéressant, n.m.*) : A graphic organizer that encourages students to analyse information, identify positive or negative aspects of the topic, then draw conclusions.

Portfolio (*Portfolio, n.m*) : A purposeful collection of student work that tells the story of their efforts, progress, and achievement.

professional learning community (*communauté d'apprentissage professionnel, n.f.*) : A group of educators sharing a common vision who collaboratively engage in professional development using reflective practice.

proficiency (*compétence, n.f.*) : Student advancement in knowledge or skill in the language.

project-based learning (*apprentissage par projets, n.m.*) : An approach centered on the completion of a project or task at the end of a learning sequence.

pronunciation (*prononciation, n.f.*) : The act or manner of pronouncing a word.

purposeful oral language (*communication orale favorisant un usage authentique de la langue, n.f.*) : Use of language to communicate a meaningful message that connects with students' lives.

questioning techniques (*techniques de questionnement, n.f.pl.*) : Instructional skill whereby the teacher frames questions to accomplish a specific learning goal and to meet the various learning needs of students.

reader's theatre (*théâtre lu, n.m.*) : A dramatic reading of a text that allows for scripts and some props, but does not involve a stage, full costumes, or memorization.

real audience (*public cible authentique, n.m.*) : Students prepare their project or task for an audience outside the classroom: other classes, parents, or adults in the community.

real-life task (*tâche authentique, n.f.*) : See authentic task.

reflection (*réflexion, n.f.*) : A form of self-assessment whereby students reflect on content or on ways of learning content.

reflective practitioner (*praticien réfléchi, n.m.*) : Teachers who make themselves aware of ongoing research in education, use research to modify their practices, and continually refine their skills through self-reflection.

representing (*représentation, n.f.*) : A production skill, which may involve speaking, drawing, or writing to present an idea or respond to text.

Retelling and Role Play (*Narration, n.f., et Jeu de rôles, n.m.*) : Activities in which students recount a text in a new way or play the roles of characters to dramatize a text.

scaffolding (*étayage, n.m.*) : Supports provided by the teacher to help students attain a more advanced level of skills and knowledge.

self-directed learning (*apprentissage autodirigé, n.m.*) : A process in which learners analyse their learning needs, formulate goals, select appropriate learning strategies, and reflect on and evaluate their learning.

Sentence Starters and Models (*Débuts de phrases et modèles, loc.*) : A tactic that provides students with support as they learn to formulate their own responses to questions and situations.

shared assessment (*évaluation partagée, n.f.*) : An assessment tool that provides space for student self-assessment, teacher assessment, and feedback from a parent or guardian.

shared practice (*démonstration partagée, n.f.*) : The second of four incremental steps in the gradual release of responsibility model. The teacher models a task for students with student involvement.

shared reading (*lecture partagée, n.f.*) : Students see the text, listen to an expert reading it with fluency and expression, and may be invited to read along.

sound-symbol relationships (*rapports sons et symboles, loc.*) : Patterns between a sound or phoneme and the symbols or letters of the alphabet used to represent that sound.

Story Map (*Schéma du récit, n.m.*) : Key elements of a text are visually represented to show the connections and relationships among them.

strategic tools (*techniques associées aux stratégies, n.f.pl.*) : Tactics and graphic organizers that help students make meaning and organize their thinking.

strategy (*stratégie, n.f.*) : Technique used by students or teachers to accomplish or facilitate a meaning-making task.

template (*modèle, n.m.*) : Model that acts as a guide for students to follow as they substitute their own words and sentences.

text (*texte, n.m.*) : A representation of ideas in many formats: aural, audiovisual, electronic, graphic, or written.

text analyser and critic (*analyste de texte, n.m.f.*) : One of the four roles of the literate student: the student provides global responses to text (e.g., opinions, inferences, etc.).

text features (*format du texte, n.m.*) : Elements of a text, such as headings, subtitles, and illustrations, used to contextualize the text.

text user (*utilisateur de texte, n.m.*) : One of the four roles of the literate student: the student uses text to communicate aural, visual, and written messages.

think-aloud (*penser tout haut, loc.*) : The teacher verbalizes the thought processes involved in accomplishing a task.

time and intensity (*temps consacré à l'enseignement du FLS et intensité du programme, loc.*) : Factors
that influence the level of proficiency of FSL students.

Timeline (*Ligne de temps, n.f.*) : Graphic organizer used to summarize informative text or biographies.

toolkit (*boîte à outils, n.f.*) : Resources available to the student for working with language.

total physical response (*réponse physique au langage oral, n.f.*) : Instructional strategy whereby students respond to commands that require physical movement, thereby strengthening the connections in the brain between new words or phrases and their meaning.

Traffic Light (*Signalisation, n.f.*) : Tactic whereby students point to a disc or other object featuring the colours of a stoplight to indicate their level of understanding.

Venn Diagram (*Diagramme de Venn, n.m.*) : A graphic organizer that invites students to look for logical relationships, similarities, and differences between pieces of information.

vocabulary bank (*banque de vocabulaire, n.f.*) : A personal dictionary created by students containing words linked to a particular theme.

Web blog (*blogue sur Internet, n.m.*) : A Web site where personal entries on a particular subject may be displayed.

word family (*famille de mots, n.f.*) : Groups of words that share a common root linking them together.

Word Sorts (*Triages de mots, n.m.pl.*) : A tactic that requires students to group together words in variable ways according to patterns.

Word Wall (*Mur de mots, n.m.*) : A display or grouping of theme- or topic-related words, serving as a reference to students during a learning sequence.

Word Web (*Toile de mots, n.f.*) : A tactic used to record vocabulary and show relationships between words.

Zone of Proximal Development (*Zone proximale de développement, n.f.*) : The cognitive region that lies between what students can do independently and what they cannot do, even with maximum assistance.

Appendix C: References and Further Reading

Ways to Use this Resource

Atwell, N. *The Thoughtful Practitioner in Side by Side*. Portsmouth, NH: Heinemann, 1992.

Carr, W. "Canada's Bilingualism Ideal: A Case Study of Intensive French in British Columbia." (Doctoral Dissertation) Burnaby, BC: Simon Fraser University, 2007.

Lapkin, S., MacFarlane, A., and Vandergrift, L. *Teaching French in Canada: FSL Teachers' Perspectives*. Ottawa, ON: Canadian Teachers' Federation, 2006.

Lewis, C. "A Little Off Balance: Exploring Teachers' Experiences with a Communicative-Experiential Curriculum in French as a Second Language Through Teacher Inquiry." (Doctoral Dissertation) Burnaby, BC: Simon Fraser University, 1995.

Serafini, F. *Building Capacity for Literacy Instruction* [Instructional DVD]. Toronto, ON: Pearson Education Canada, 2006.

Serafini, F. *Lessons in Comprehension Professional e-Book* [Interactive CD]. Toronto, ON: Pearson Education Canada, 2006.

Stoll, L., Fink, D., and Earl, L. *It's About Learning (and It's About Time)*. Oxford, UK: Routledge, 2003.

Turnbull, M. "Multidimensional Project-based Teaching in Core French: A Case Study." (Doctoral Dissertation) University of Toronto, 1998.

Wells, G. *Changing Schools From Within: Creating Communities of Inquiry*. Portsmouth, NH: Heinemann, 1994.

Setting the Context: Literacy in FSL

Atlantic Provinces Education Foundation (APEF). Halifax, NS: APEF, 1996.

BC Ministry of Education. Core French Integrated Resource Package. Victoria, BC, 2001.

Bournot-Trites, M. and Tellowitz, U. *Report of Current Research on the Effects of Second Language Learning on First Language Literacy Skills.* Halifax, NS: APEF, 2002.

Carr, W. "Intensive French: A British Columbia Perspective." *Canadian Parents for French Bulletin* (Winter 2007): 8–9.

Cook, V. "Linguistics and Second Language Acquisition: One Person with Two Languages." Edited by Aronoff and Rees-Miller, *Blackwell Handbook of Linguistics.* Oxford, UK: Blackwell, 2000.

Cummins, J., Brown, K., and Sayers, D. *Literacy, Technology, and Diversity: Teaching for Success in Changing Times.* Boston, MA: Allyn & Bacon, 2007.

Elley, W. "Acquiring Literacy in a Second Language: The Effect of Book-based Programs." *Language Learning* 41 (1991): 375–411.

Freebody, P. "A Socio-Cultural Approach: Resourcing Four Roles as a Literacy Learner." In Watson, A. and Badenhop, A. (Eds.). *Prevention of Reading Failure.* Gosford: Ashton Scholastic, 1992.

Genesee, F. and Cloud, N. *Multilingualism is Basic. Educational Leadership* 55, no. 6 (1998): 62–65.

Germain, C. and Netten, J. "Introduction: Intensive French." *Canadian Modern Language Review* 60, no. 3 (2004): 263–273.

Guthrie, J. "Teaching for Literacy Engagement." *Journal of Literacy Research* 36, no. 1 (2004): 1–30.

Krashen, S. *The Power of Reading.* Westport, CT: Libraries Unlimited, 2004.

Literacy for Learning: The Report of the Expert Panel on Literacy in Grades 4–6 in Ontario, December, 2004.

Luke, A. and Freebody, P. "Literacies Programs: Debates and Demands in Cultural Context." *Prospect: Australian Journal of TESOL* 5, no. 7 (1990): 7–16.

Ontario Ministry of Education and Training, Ontario, 1998.

New London Group. *A Pedagogy of Multiliteracies: Designing Social Futures.* Cambridge, MA: ©1996 by the President and Fellows of Harvard College.

Swain, M., Lapkin, S., Rowen, N., and Hart, D. *The Role of Mother Tongue Literacy in Third Language Learning* 4 (1990): 111–21.

Turnbull, M. "Multidimensional Project-based Second Language Teaching: Observations of Four Grade 9 Core French Teachers." In Lapkin, S. and Turnbull, M. (Eds.) Research in FSL Education: The State of the Art. *Canadian Modern Language Review* (Special Issue), 56, no. 1(1999): 3–35.

Turnbull, M., Lapkin, S., and Hart, D. "Grade 3 Immersion Students: Performance in Literacy and Mathematics: Province-wide Results from Ontario (1998/99)." *Canadian Modern Language Review* 58, no. 1 (2001).

UNESCO, Statement for the United Nations Literacy Decade, 2003–2012.

Big Idea 1
Motivating and Engaging Students: Making It Real

Allington, R. "What I've Learned about Effective Reading Instruction from a Decade of Studying Exemplary Elementary Classroom Teachers." *Phi Delta Kappan* 83, no. 10 (2002): 740–747.

Atlantic Provinces Education Foundation. Halifax, NS: APEF, 2003.

Bransford, J., Brown, A., and Cocking, R. *How People Learn: Brain, Mind, Experience, and School.* Washington, DC: National Academy Press, 2001.

CASLT *National Core French Study: A Model for Implementation*. Ottawa, ON: Canadian Association of Second Language Teachers, 1994.

Cummins, J. "The Role of Primary Language Development in Promoting Educational Success for Language Minority Students." *Schooling and Language Minority Students: A Theoretical Framework*. Los Angeles: California State University: Evaluation, Dissemination, and Assessment Center, 1981.

Cummins, J., Brown, K., and Sayers, D. *Literacy, Technology, and Diversity: Teaching for Success in Changing Times*. Boston, MA: Allyn & Bacon, 2007.

Dörnyei, Z. *Teaching and Researching Motivation*. London, UK: Pearson Education, 2001.

Fried-Booth, D. *Project Work*. Oxford, UK: Oxford University Press, 1986.

Gardner, R., Lalonde, R., and Moorcroft, R. "The Role of Attitudes and Motivation in Second Language Learning: Correlational and Experimental Considerations." *Language Learning* 35 (1985): 207–227.

Hedge, T. 1993. "Project Work." *ELT Journal* 47, no. 3 (1993): 276–277.

Jeroski, S. *Literacy in Action* ProGuide™. Toronto, ON: Pearson Education Canada, 2007.

Knutson, E. "Reading with a Purpose: Communicative Reading Tasks for the Foreign Language Classroom." *Foreign Language Annals* 30, no. 1 (1997).

Krashen, Stephen D. *The Power of Reading: Insights from the Research*. Portsmouth, NH: Heinemann, 2004.

Legutke, M. and Thomas. H. *Process and Experience in the Language Classroom*. Harlow, UK: Longman, 1991.

Tremblay, R., Duplantie, M., and Huot, D. "The Communicative/Experiential Syllabus. The National Core French Study." Ottawa: Canadian Association of Second Language Teachers, 1990: 58–59.

Van Duzer, C. *Reading and the Adult English Language Learner.* Washington, DC: Clearinghouse for ESL Literacy Education, 1999.

Vygotsky, L. *Thought and Language*. In E. Hanfmann and G. Vakar (Eds. & Trans.). *Thought and Language*. Cambridge, MA: MIT Press, 1962.

Big Idea 2
Integrating Oral Language: Communicating for Success

Fountas I. and Pinnell G. *Guiding Readers and Writers*: *Teaching Comprehension, Genre, and Content Literacy*. Portsmouth, NH: Heinemann, 2001.

Jeroski, S. *Reaching Readers: Canadian Biographies*. Teacher's Guide and Transparency Pack. Toronto, ON: Pearson Education Canada, 2005.

Pearson, P. and Gallagher, M. "The Instruction of Reading Comprehension." *Contemporary Educational Psychology*, 8 (1983).

Routman, R. *Reading Essentials: The Specifics You Need to Teach Reading Well*. Portsmouth, NH: Heinemann, 2003.

Tremblay, R. "National Core French Study Summary Report." *Bulletin de Langues Secondes.* Ottawa, ON: CASLT, 1990.

Turnbull, M. "There is a Role for the L1 in Second and Foreign Language Teaching." *Canadian Modern Language Review* 57 (2001): 531–540.

Big Idea 3
Developing Language Awareness: Discovering Patterns

Beers K., Probst R., and Rief L. *Adolescent Literacy: Turning Promise into Practice.* Portsmouth, NH: Heinemann, 2007.

Hill S. *Developing early Literacy: Assessment and Teaching.* Prahran, AU: 2006.

Luke, A. and Freebody, P. "Literacies Programs: Debates and Demands in Cultural Context." *Prospect: Australian Journal of TESOL* 5, no. 7 (1990): 7–16.

Big Idea 4
Assessing and Differentiating: Reaching All Learners

Bennett, B. and Rolheiser, C. *Beyond Monet: The Artful Science of Instructional Integration.* Toronto, ON: Bookation Inc., 2001.

Black, P., Harrison, C., Lee, C., Marshall, B., and Wiliam, D. "Working Inside the Black Box: Assessment for Learning in the Classroom." *Phi Delta Kappan* 86, no. 1 (September 2004): 9–21.

Cummins, J., Brown, K., and Sayers, D. *Literacy, Technology, and Diversity: Teaching for Success in Changing Times.* Boston, MA: Allyn & Bacon, 2006.

Gardner, H. *Multiple Intelligences: The Theory in Practice.* New York, NY: Basic Books, 1993.

McCarthy, B. *The 4Mat System: Teaching to Learning Styles with Right/Left Mode Techniques.* Thousand Oaks, CA: Corwin Press, 1981.

Ontario Ministry of Education. *Education for All: The Report of the Expert Panel on Literacy and Numeracy Instruction for Students with Special Education Needs, Kindergarten to Grade 6.* Toronto, ON: Queen's Printer, 2005.

Paradis, J., Nicoladis, E., and Genesee, F. "Early Emergence of Structural Constraints on Code-Mixing: Evidence from French-English Bilingual Children." *Bilingualism: Language and Cognition*, vol. 3 (2000).

Sousa, D. Presentation. Interactive Innovations Conference. Vancouver, BC: Ministry of Education, 2007.

Stiggins, R. Presentation. *Through the Eyes of the Learner Conference.* Winnipeg, MB: Teachers' Society, 2003.

Stiggins, R. "Assessment Crisis: The Absence of Assessment FOR Learning." *Phi Delta Kappan* 83, no. 10 (2002): 758–765.

Tomlinson, C. *How to Differentiate Instruction in Mixed-ability Classrooms.* 2nd ed. Alexandria, VA: ASCD, 2001.

Big Idea 5
Activating Strategies: Making Connections

Beck, I. and McKeown, M. "Developing Questions that Promote Comprehension: The Story Map." *Language Arts* 58 (1981): 913–918.

Bennett, I., Rolheiser, C., and Stevahn, L. *Cooperative Learning: Where Heart Meets Mind.* Toronto, ON: Educational Connections, 1991.

Carr, E. and Ogle, D. "K-W-L Plus: A Strategy for Comprehension and Summarization." *Journal of Reading* 30, no. 7 (1987): 626–631.

Chamot, Anna U. *Teaching Learning Strategies to Foreign Students.* Washington, DC: Center for Applied Linguistics, 1998.

Cummins, J. *Bilingualism and Special Education: Issues in Assessment and Pedagogy.* San Diego, CA: College Hill Press, 1984.

Cummins, J. *Negotiating Identities: Education for Empowerment in a Diverse Society.* Ontario, CA: California Association for Bilingual Education, 1995.

Cummins, J. *Negotiating Identities: Education for Empowerment in a Diverse Society* (2nd ed.). Los Angeles, CA: California Association for Bilingual Education, 2001.

Cummins, J. "Teaching the Language of Social Studies." *Leadership Letters: Issues and Trends in Social Studies.* Toronto, ON: Pearson Education Canada, 2006.

Daniel, M. "Helping Linguistic Minorities Read Independently." *Academic Exchange Quarterly 9*, no. 2 (2005): 1–9.

Flavell, J. "Metacognition and Cognitive Monitoring: A New Area of Cognitive-Developmental Inquiry." *American Psychologist* 34 (1979): 906–911.

Herber, H. *Teaching Reading in Content Areas.* 2nd ed. Englewood Cliffs, NJ: Prentice-Hall, 1978.

Hoffman, J. "Critical Reading/Thinking Across the Curriculum: Using I-charts to Support Learning." *Language Arts* 69 (1992): 121–127.

Krashen, S. *Principles and Practice in Second Language Learning and Acquisition.* Oxford, UK: Pergamon, 1982.

Oxford, R. *Language Learning Strategies: What Every Teacher Should Know.* New York, NY: Newbury House, 1990.

Reyes, M. "Unleashing Possibilities: Biliteracy in the Primary Grades." In Reyes, M. and Halcón, J. (Eds.), *The best for our children: Critical perspectives on literacy for Latino students.* New York, NY: Teachers College Press, 2001: 96–121.

Scarcella, R. and Oxford, R. *The Tapestry of Language Learning: The Individual in the Communicative Classroom.* Boston, MA: Heinle and Heinle Publishers, 1992.

Swain, M. "Communicative Competence: Some Roles of Comprehensible Input and Comprehensible Output in its Development." In Gass, S. and Madden, C. (Eds.), *Input in Second Language Acquisition*, pp. 235–256. New York, NY: Newbury House, 1985.

Swain, M. "The Output Hypothesis and Beyond: Mediating Acquisition Through Collaborative Dialogue." In J. Lantolf (Ed.), *Sociocultural Theory and Second Language Learning*, pp. 97–114. Oxford, UK: Oxford University Press, 2000.

Vygotsky, L. *Thought and Language.* In E. Hanfmann and G. Vakar (Eds. & Trans.). *Thought and Language.* Cambridge, MA: MIT Press, 1962.

Vygotsky, L. *Mind in Society* (Eds. & Trans.: Cole, M., John-Steiner, V., Scribner, S., and Souberman, E.). Cambridge, MA: Harvard University Press, 1978.

Appendix D: Index

action research, 13, 14, 15

anticipation, 39, 42

assessment, 54–61

    assessment for learning, 54–56, 57, 75, 79, 85, 91, 95, 99, 105, 109

    assessment of learning, 56

    cycle, 57

    opportunities, 55

    reflection, 60, 70, 75, 76, 79,81, 85, 88, 91, 92, 95, 96, 99, 101, 105, 106, 109, 110

Bloom's Taxonomy, 40

cognates and familiar words, 49–50

communicative-experiential approach, 19

communicative language teaching (CLT), 9

comprehension strategies

    overview of, 72–73

    ask questions, 74–77

    make predictions, 78–83

    monitor and repair comprehension, 84–89

    make connections, 90–93

    visualize, 94–97

    summarize, 98–103

    synthesize, 104–107

    analyse and evaluate, 108–111

contextualization, 39, 42

critical thinking, 19

culture

    cultural identities, 31–33, 64–65

differentiated instruction, 54–61

    cycle, 57

Dual-iceberg Theory, 64

engagement and motivation, 26–35

FSL

    definition, 18

Gradual Release of Responsibility, 38, 72–73

graphic organizer, 67–68, 112–142

input hypothesis, 65

    output, 65

in-service programs, 16

instructional tactics, 112–142

Intensive French, 21

language

    awareness, 47

    breaking the code, 47

    forms of, 47

    keeping the focus in perspective, 46

    structures, 51–52

    tools, 48

learning styles, 58, 59

literacy

    cognitive, 66–67

    definition of, 18–19, 24

    environment, 33–34

    learning continuum, 63, 66

    linking first and second language, 21, 62

    literacy skills, 62–63, 66

    metacognitive, 66–67

    strategies, 66

literacy teacher, 34

literate learner

    the four roles, 19–20

metacognition

    strategies, 66–67

    skills, 68

multiliteracies, 23–24

multimodal approach, 24

multiple intelligences, 54, 58–59

oral language

    purposeful, 36–45

personalization, 39, 42

pre-service programs, 16

prior knowledge, 44, 62–64

professional learning communities, 13

professional learning survey, 16, 17, 25, 35, 45, 53, 61, 71

projects and tasks (project-based learning), 26, 28–29

reflective practice (practitioners), 12, 13, 14

scaffolding, 22, 29, 38, 63, 66

second language learning

    principles of learning, 22

    benefits of, 23

self-directed learning, 13

shared reading, 40, 43

sound-symbol relationships, 48–49

text

    choosing texts, 29–31

    types of, 28

    identifying a purpose for, 32

Think Aloud, 73

word family, 50–51

Zone of Proximal Development, 29, 63

Notes

Notes

Notes

Notes

effective literacy practices in **FSL: making connections**